And Then I Heard His Voice

by Eli Contreras

And Then I Heard His Voice
by Eli Contreras

Printed in the United States of America

ISBN 9781615795550

www.xulonpress.com

Dedication

ᘛᘚ

This book is dedicated to Jesus Christ, the Lover and Lifter of my soul…the One who gave His life so that I could have life.

To my father Eulalio Contreras for being the man God gave me as a father, to my mother Dominga Contreras who never gave up on me, and to my very patient brother and two sisters.

In loving memory of Demetrius Contreras, Maria A. Tobar, and Cesar Elizarraz.

Acknowledgements

I would like to thank Pastor Dorine Younger and my family in Christ at the Arms of Compassion Worship Center for all their prayers and support. I would like to extend this acknowledgement to include Pastor Will Franco from Canto Nuevo Ministries, Pastor Roland, Mirza Catalan from Impacto Espiritual Church, Roger and Miriam Sobalvarro, Cheryl Cox, Anne Marie Ritchie, W.Joseph Schlitt, Ione Maddox, George Jeffers, and Doug and Margaret Boyd.

Thank you to Barbara Fry for organizing and putting my thoughts and random writings on the written page.

My gratitude also goes to Jesus Campos for using the God-given inspiration and talent to create the amazing cover of this book.

To everyone who prayed and believed God to restore my life and everyone who God placed in and through my life, thank you. And to all those who offered their help and support, technical advice, and encouragement in this project, I am very grateful, and God bless you.

Introduction

ꟷ

As a little boy, I was plagued by demons, my father abused me, and I was rejected by most of my peers. At times, I had to fight everyday to exist the best way I knew how. I had a lot of pain, which I tried to deaden with drugs. I lived to get high, and I did whatever I had to do to survive. Getting high was the meaning of my existence, and it led me into a downward spiral that caused me to experience many close calls that could have led to my death.

I have omitted and changed the names of the people in this book in order to protect their privacy.

Some of the story may not seem to be in perfect order, because I was pretty transient. There were times that I stayed in one place at one time, then soon after, I would go to another. At times, I would stay in a garage, an abandoned car, then a park bench, and next, a bush. I was all over the place. Moreover, there were times when some things that I have talked about would later remind me of something else, and they were added to the text.

Actually, there are many things that I don't remember at all. I am aware that I was mentally ill, and there are blanks in my life that I cannot recall. A lot of people have told me things that I did, but I have no idea of what they were talking about.

This is a story about my life that I have told as well as I can remember.

Chapter I

Into Unknown Darkness

ꕥ

We ran through the cut fence and slid down into a broad, tree-lined creek bed. Splashing through meandering, algae- filled pools, we tried to catch our breath as we ran. Soon, we came upon a large, silver pipe that captured the waters and ominously disappeared underground.

"Come on! In here! In the sewer!" my friend cried.

I remember frantically looking down the long, dark pipe thinking that there was no way I wanted to go in it without knowing where I was headed or where I would come out.

Similarly, that was what was happening in my life, as I was later to see.

But I really didn't have any choice…it was either run into the unknown darkness of the sewer or be beaten up by some older kids. So I followed my friend as he disappeared into the black abyss.

"Wait up!" I yelled, gasping as I ran. I was sweating bullets.

We sloshed through the dirty creek water that coursed through the middle of the flood control pipe. I could barely see my friend's outline as he continued to run ahead of me in the dark. I wondered how I could have gotten myself into so much trouble!

I was in second grade, and I lived in Pittsburg, California with my father, mother, two brothers, and my sister. My dad had moved us there in order to be near his job as a custodian at Los Medanos Community College. We lived in a modest, tan and brown apartment that was part of a large complex, not too far from a Catholic Church and about two miles from my school. My older sister is two years older than I am, and seven years later, my younger sister was born.

I shared a bedroom with my eldest brother, who is four years older, and another brother, three years my elder. I remember how the youngest of my brothers told me that sometimes when he went to sleep, he would see an angel floating in the corner of the room close to where he slept on the top section of the bunk bed.

Every year, the school had a Halloween parade where all the kids would dress up in costumes and walk around the schoolyard. Everyone could hardly wait until the day of the parade. But our family didn't have the money to buy me a costume. So while others excitedly got in line to show off their outfits, I had to stay in the classroom and sit in my seat. My desk was in front of the window, facing the direction of my home. I sat there during the parade hoping that I would see my mother walking up to the school with a costume. But that never happened.

While my parents were at work, my aunt cared for us after school. I considered my aunt to be my second mom. She would teach us how to read and sing songs. Sometimes, we would play school, and she would be the teacher. My aunt would ask us questions, and if we knew the answers, we would have to raise our hands just like in the classroom. Sometimes, we would play "Disco", and she would line us all up and we would have fun dancing to her favorite songs. She had us learn the words so that we could sing along. When we got hungry, we pretended like it was lunchtime, and she would cook food and serve it just like it was a cafeteria.

Sometimes, if we misbehaved or didn't listen in "class", she would grab the little paddle that used to have an elastic band and a rubber ball at the end. Sometimes, we would make her chase us just for fun. One time, she chased my brother up the stairs and broke the paddle on his backside, but he got away, and we all laughed.

I had a friend who was in the fourth grade. We were the youngest sons of the only families in the school who were not African American. There was a high school across the street, and after the schools let out, some of the older boys would come over to pick up siblings or in my case, settle a score.

Members of my family got along well within the complex community, until one of the kids spread a rumor that I had been making racial remarks about some others there. It wasn't true, but he was jealous that we all got along so well. It wasn't too long before some high school kids came over to my school to get revenge. It didn't matter that I was just seven years old.

On that particular day when I came out of school, I noticed a group of high school boys slowly strolling over my way. As they walked closer and closer, I could hear them making fun of me and cussing. My friend and his older brother, who was in the sixth grade, moved in to defend me.

"Take him through the sewer!" the older brother exclaimed, trying to fend them off.

He stayed there and fought them off as best he could while his younger brother helped me make my escape.

We ran as fast as we could through the muddy creek, into the opening of a flood control system, and through the long, black and damp labyrinth of pipes. It was scary, but he was a good guide as he had been through it before. I couldn't turn back, and since there was no other choice, I just kept going. Amazingly, after about twenty minutes, we emerged back into the daylight near my apartment, a couple miles from the school.

For most of my life, I traveled through a maze of dark and frightening experiences. Later, when I got into drugs, I truly had tunnel vision, only seeing what I wanted to see. I didn't care about anything else going on around me; all I wanted to do was to get high. It wasn't until years later that I would be guided out of that black existence and into light.

The Shed

After hearing about this incident at school, my mother said that that was enough! My oldest brother had already moved out because he didn't like the racial problems. With the new baby and all that was going on, my mother convinced my father that this was not a safe place to live. One morning, she told us kids to pack up so we could leave. We moved everything out that same day! We piled everything into a two-toned "hippie" van, and drove to my grandmother's house in Oakley.

My grandmother had a somewhat large, country home, and my uncle and his wife, another aunt, and two cousins lived there with her. There wasn't room for our family to stay in her house, but she had a small shed in the back. Since we had no other place to go, we gratefully moved in. We would be safe there!

The shed was just one room that was made of wood, about 10' x 8', with no insulation. It had one door and two windows. There was one bed for my parents and a small tv. All of our clothes were piled up in the corner, and my brothers, sisters, and I slept on the floor with blankets. We ate in the main house and also went there to use the bathroom. We existed in these cramped quarters for two months.

My father still had his job at the college, and my mother worked at a seasonal job picking tomatoes in the large fields in the area. She rode on the large harvester where a row of people were lined up on one side and then on the other. Work on this machine was long, tedious, and potentially dangerous. My mother told about a lady who became so excited and distracted that family members were coming out to give her a birthday cake that she accidentally got her hand caught in the angry jaws of the machinery and was pulled into it. Tragically, she died. Another one of my aunts also worked on the machine. The accident affected her so much that she went on to complete her education and become a social worker for the county.

My aunt (by marriage) planted some beautiful, fluffy, yellow and orange marigolds in the front and sides of my grandmother's house. We kids thought they were so pretty that we wanted some, too. So, what did we do? We waited until no one was looking, dug up all her flowers, gingerly carried them to the back, and replanted them all around the shed! My aunt didn't really get upset, but she thought that we didn't like her and that we were trying to be mean. But we didn't have any bad feelings towards her. We just wanted our shed to look nice.

One day while my parents were at work, we went out into the backyard to play. We were giggling, running, and chasing each other like all kids do. My grandmother didn't speak English, and when she heard us laughing and carrying on outside, she thought we were making fun of her. She told my uncle that we were teasing her.

My uncle liked to drink, and he often drank too much. Drunk and outraged, he burst out of the house, ran over to us, and started slapping us around with the back of his hand.

When my mother came home from work, we told her what had happened. She was appalled!

I remember her saying, "If we have to stay in the van, we have to stay in the van; but we're not staying here any more!"

The next thing we knew, we were in the car again, looking for a new place to live.

The Projects

My thoughts drifted to where we used to live in Oakley when I was four. It was in the "Projects".

The Projects was a collection of modest, cream-colored stucco duplexes, not too far from the Sheriff's substation, the Catholic church, and the local Mexican market. Each house had two bedrooms, one bath, and little back yard with a clothesline and grass. Ivy surrounded the chain-linked fences that cut through the adjacent yards, and there was an open field in the back.

I vividly recall our morning routine. I always woke up early, and it would still be dark outside. My father would be in the living room drinking coffee and watching Mr. Ed, a tv sit com about a man who owned a talking horse. My mother would be in the kitchen fixing his lunch. Then, Dad would leave for work. Although this sounds like a typical morning for a pre-school kid, there was much more in my life that was not normal. I should have had a happy, carefree childhood, but I did not.

My family often struggled emotionally, physically, and spiritually. I am sure that my mother hid many problems from us, but she was and still is a wonderful mother, and she always tried hard to make things right and to make them work.

Unlike some men who abandoned their families or would leave for long periods of time, my father was at home. And he was a good provider; he earned the money to buy basic food and clothes, but really nothing more. There was not enough for extras, and sometimes, it was hard to make ends meet (well, of course, we could have had more if money had not been spent on alcohol).

Nevertheless, he wasn't a good father to us; he was an alcoholic. Moreover, he never really attempted to have a good relationship with us. He didn't really talk to us. The only time he spoke was when he was drunk. But as a young child, I didn't really know that. And as a result, I accepted my father's actions as normal. He was my dad, and I knew him all my life. But as a human being, I can't say that I knew him at all.

Sometimes, my father would get so drunk and so out of control that my mother would rush us out of the house and into the van. It would take him a minute to realize that we were leaving, but I still remember how we all scrambled to get into the car. Then, Mom would close our door and run around to get in. I remember looking at her and turning toward the house as if in a horror movie. I could just anticipate that a monster that would appear at any moment. Then, she would start up the van, and the sound gave us away. I would see the front door fly open and my father bursting out at full speed. I'll never forget his scary face. As she put the car into gear and began to pull away, Dad threw himself on the side of the car and screamed like a madman. My siblings and I shifted over to the other side of the car to escape the monster, but in reality, it was no game and that monster was my father.

On the weekends, my father would often get together with some of his drinking buddies, usually my aunt and uncle and the neighbors who lived directly across from us, and they would drink, listen to music, and dance. But it only took a few drinks before things got out of control. Before you knew it, fists were flying and bottles were breaking. Sometimes, it would be one on one, and other times, it would be an all out brawl. But regardless, it was crazy! Furniture would be turned over, things would be breaking, and people would be beating each other up. They were punching, ripping out each other's hair, tearing clothes, screaming, and desperately swinging and grabbing each other as if they were trying to kill each other. The fights usually started at the kitchen table, but as they became more heated and violent, they moved into the living room. Then, the craziness somehow ended up outside. Although there was always someone there to hustle all of us kids into another room so we wouldn't see the fighting, we saw plenty! And what we didn't see, we could hear.

I guess my parents used to drink as a way to relax and get their minds off of life for a while, but it just seemed to add to their problems. After being visited by the police many times, the officers gave my parents an ultimatum: either stop drinking or the next time, we will take your kids. That was all my mom needed to hear. She chose her kids over the bottle and never drank again. As for my dad, he continued full speed ahead.

Mom was always a wonderful mother. She always took good care of us kids. She always helped us when we got hurt, and she was very protective of us, even from my father.

One day while running after my brother, I ran into the grass area in front of the house. Just then, I felt pressure on my foot. When I looked down, I saw that my foot was all red! I ran inside screaming for my mother and leaving a trail of blood behind me.

When she saw me, she picked me up in a panic yelling, "What happened?"

She rushed me into the bathroom, put me in the bathtub, and turned on the water. It didn't take long for the tub water to turn a bright shade of crimson. I remember the look of panic on my mom's face as she ran out of the room, grabbed the keys, and started the car. She then ran back into the bathroom, but when she saw all the blood, she started screaming words in Spanish that I didn't understand. She pulled me out of the tub, wrapped my foot in a towel, and carried me to the car. My dad was just coming home from work. Seeing the panic on our faces, he threw down his lunch pale and asked what had happened. My mother explained that I cut my foot and that she had to take me to the hospital. For some reason, my father became infuriated, and he took off his belt and started swinging at me while I was still in my mother's arms. Using her body to push past him, she got me to the car and threw me in the back seat. She was able to drive away from him, and she rushed me to the hospital, which was just down the street at the time. The blood soaked through the towel and made a puddle on the car seat during the short time it took us to get there. But I was o.k. They sewed up my foot, and it later healed up nicely.

While other children enjoyed going out and doing things with their families, we usually stayed at home. My parents never really took us anywhere except for occasional trips to the river. Realizing the need for family bonding, my mother would ask my father to take us somewhere so we could be together. Finally, Dad would agree to take us to the park on weekends, and Mom would get us kids all dressed up and ready to go. But then, he'd say he would be right back. When he returned, he'd be drunk! As a result, we wouldn't go anywhere. My mother didn't want to go any place with him, because he would get loud and threaten people. I remember that my brothers and I would have to pull him away from people he had threatened. The others would see that his kids (even a little kid like me) were present, so for the sake of family, they didn't fight back. We were embarrassed and ashamed, not to mention scared. I'm sure that the people could see the fear in our eyes. It was like we had to baby sit my father. So, we usually stayed home. But then, his buddies would come over, the drinking would begin, and the fighting would start all over again.

My family got together for festive, delicious Mexican food, traditions, and colorful birthday and holiday celebrations. There would be cousins, aunts and uncles, and their families. On Christmas, we'd all gather at my grandmother's house and celebrate. We used to all help out and make tamales while the family would visit. Later at night, we would all open presents.

For Easter, we would go to my uncle's house. They would set up their yard and bar-b-qued hamburgers, hot dogs, and chicken. There would be different kinds of salads, drinks, and, of course, delicious pastries. After everyone ate and was full, all the grownups would hide the eggs so that all the children could hunt for them. Christmas and Easter were usually the only two times that the whole family got together. After my grandmother died, Christmas was never the same. A lot of the happiness went away. Each family celebrated in their own ways at their own houses. And honestly, there wasn't too much brightness in my life.

Often, there wasn't enough money to celebrate birthdays. One year, it was my birthday. I was waiting all day for a present or a surprise, but I didn't get anything. Finally, at night, my mom brought me a piece of sweet bread and said, "Happy Birthday." That was all she could do.

While in the Projects, my cousin and I were accepted into the Headstart program, which is designed to start children who may need language or other skills at a young age so that they will have a greater chance to succeed in school. However, we really didn't know how to get along with other kids.

One day, I was playing with of pail of dirt. A kid came up and took my pail. I started to wail.

My cousin ran over to me and asked, "What happened?"

"He took my dirt!" I cried.

My cousin immediately stormed over to the boy and punched him repeatedly. Then he brought my dirt back to me.

As a result, my cousin and I were sent home.

At other times, another boy and I would destroy school materials that were on the table or shelves. I don't know why I wanted to do that, but perhaps I was acting out as a result of some of the things that were happening in my life. We would break and crush crayons, crayon holders, and pencils, and spread glue around. We were finally suspended. Suspended from pre-school! What an accomplishment! That kind of set the tone for my future in school.

Across the street from the Projects was a big hole or swamp that used to fill with water in the winter when it rained. It could have been dangerous if it had been very deep, but it was more wide than tall. The lure of all that wonderful mud was just too much for us kids. So we crossed the street, made a b-line towards the hole, and had great fun playing and getting covered from head to toe in the slimy ooze... that is, until my mother came out with a stick in her hand. We started to cry, because we knew that she would use it. Then, we ran. We split in all directions, but she chased us around and around with that stick. The neighbor kids doubled over laughing.

Another memory I have of living in the Projects had to do with a kitchen table. Down the street from the Sheriff's substation and across the main highway, there was a split-level Mexican market, where the downstairs was in the back. They used to hand out free food to the needy downstairs.

One day, my uncle collected a lot of the food in Styrofoam cartons, brought it to our house, and set it on the kitchen table. All of us kids got kind of silly, and we jumped up on the table and started eating the food like little animals. It was really fun being together up there, that is, until the table broke!

My father was so mad that he sent us all to bed without any supper!

Sexual Abuse

But there were other memories that I had of living in the Projects that were a lot worse. There were the times when I was molested. Whether or not it was accepted in my father's side of the family or it was a deep, dark secret, I was sexually abused. I was four years old. And it was my father.

The same father who was supposed to nurture, shelter, protect, and teach me how to become a man was the same person that raped, destroyed, and shattered any chance of me having a normal, happy childhood.

It was like any ordinary day, and Dad took us kids to the river with some other family members and friends. My mother was at work. He had been drinking, and he carried me into the bushes and molested me. I was afraid, and I couldn't do anything to change what was happening. He was my father.

I didn't know what to do, so I just closed my eyes and wondered, "Why are you doing this?"

As a child, I used to sleep in the same bed with my parents. Sometimes, my father would molest me while my mother was asleep. I was too young to understand what was going on. I just thought it was normal. It was at that early age that I remember seeing men on tv or in a magazine, and I began to think about them in relationship to what my father had done to me.

Later on, a family friend used to come over and started spending time with me. I didn't think anything of it, because I didn't know his motives. I was just happy that someone wanted to talk to me, as I was lonely. It wasn't long before he, too, sexually abused me. This went on several times in between the ages of eight to twelve. Because my father had molested me and now this family friend, I didn't know what was appropriate behavior and what was not. I did not understand what sex was, and I would just close my eyes and wonder what had just happened.

I remember noticing men and being attracted to them at the age of five or six. I didn't know any different. Once I made sexual advances to a young boy who was visiting my brother. He told my parents on me. I remember sitting on the couch. My parents were in the kitchen, and the boy was sitting next to my brother. I knew my actions were wrong by the way that my parents looked at me, but I don't know that I was able to process it in my mind at that age.

Once in a while, some cousins from out of town would visit. My sister and I could tell that there was someone in the bedroom. When we opened the door, my cousins, who were brother and sister, were sleeping with each other. But as kids, we really didn't say anything. We just laughed and ran, acting like we didn't see them.

One time, my cousins were visiting. They were much older. We were all sleeping in the same room. In all, there about six of us: my two brothers and I and the rest cousins. The lights were out, but there were conversations going on between all of us. Suddenly through the quiet darkness, one of my cousins started laughing. Sparing no details, he then asked if anyone had ever been raped by a man. I closed my eyes hoping that someone would protect me. I thought that if I shut my eyes, I would be able to escape to another place.

Some kids don't tell adults about being abused out of fear, threats, or confusion, and there are some who do tell adults who won't listen. Sometimes women would rather keep their boyfriends or husbands than to believe their children. In my case, my mother had no idea what was going on, because I never said anything and no one else told her.

If abuse is suspected, the child needs to be encouraged to talk about it.

If a child tells someone that he or she is being molested, the responsible adult had better listen and do something about it. If they don't believe the children and help them, I guarantee they will lead shattered lives, and without the intervention of God, their lives will be destroyed.

Once I heard someone who was aware of the sexual abuse of a child confess, "I don't know what to do."

"You don't know what to do?" I asked.

"You had better do something to change the situation," I continued. "Do you know what happened to me? The same thing will happen to your child if you don't put a stop to the abuse. Your kid will self-medicate."

Demons

One time, my father told me, "Come here. I want to teach you how to pray."

He set me on his lap and started praying. But I noticed that his grip was getting tighter and tighter, and his voice got louder. Before I knew it, he was screaming, spitting, and shaking me really hard. Then, in a quiet mumble, he told me that he was the Devil and that he was going to kill me. Finally, he threw me down and walked away as if nothing happened. I didn't know what was wrong with him. He had been drinking, but it was more than that. He was being controlled by demons. They had probably tortured him as a child, as well.

After the family friend abused me, I, too, was bothered by demons. My life just seemed to be one nightmare after another. I started to experience demons talking to me, and I would see things from the corners of my eye. An extreme fear would come over me; I was afraid to sleep at night, and I couldn't be alone.

It could have been a "generational curse" or a "transfer of spirits", but all I knew was that there was a dark side to my life that turned into a real battle. I always felt that there was something inside of me that was pulling me down. It was trying to take control, and I was always trying to fight it. It was like I was trying to fight myself; it was spiritual warfare. I was controlled by demons, and I was beat up by them. I was fighting a losing battle.

Nightmares

Demons invaded my dreams. I remember being tormented by nightmares, and I tried to avoid sleeping. I vividly remember a dream that I had when I was four. It took place in a huge, eerie, haunted house that sat on a hill. It must have been five or six stories high. There were long sets of stairs that went up to the house. And on the inside, there were other staircases that went in many directions. Everything inside was blue: many shades of blue, contrasted with black. Ghosts, demons, and monsters were going up and down the stairs and all around the house. I had this dream a few times later. I knew that I was fighting the demons that were present in my life.

When I was older, I told my mother about another nightmare that I would have over and over. It was about a demon that was chasing me through an empty field. She then told me that my father would have restless nights and dream the same thing, except that he would fall down.

The demon in my dream looked human except that it didn't have skin...only chunks of meat that hung on to its bones in such a grotesque manner that it looked like it had been chewed on. I could feel it catch up with me and touch my back as I ran for my life through that field.

I also had another reoccurring nightmare. I dreamed that I was on fire and running for my life in some sort of surreal pinball machine or video game. I screamed and bounced into things that would ignite as if they were covered in gas. Then, it would explode and get hotter and hotter, and I would run on and bump into the next object. These and other dreams occurred throughout my whole life.

Later, when I was about sixteen, I had a vision, I guess you would call it. Anyway, it happened during the day. I was in a dark, mystical place, but there were no colors. It was all in different shades of black. The only light was from the lava as it flowed down the hills and waterfalls in what looked like it was once a beautiful tropical island, but everything else was just dead. Was my dream of hell?

I could hear people screaming, but I wasn't able to see anyone. I noticed that the voices were coming from an open ditch that ran right next to me. At first, I wasn't able to see much. But as the lava oozed closer over an eerie waterfall and down through the canal, I could make out that there were people in there who were chained together by the neck so that they couldn't move. The hot liquid kept moving towards them and finally flooded the entire ditch, engulfing the helpless captives who would thrash about to try to escape. But it was futile. The hot lava came every so many minutes and filled the ditch. I was able to see because of the heat of the lava gave off a reddish tint. I noticed that two demons were standing guard, watching the people burn. With morbid tools, they picked and stabbed at the people to keep them submerged under the molten liquid. They demons growled and laughed while the people screamed. It was complete evil.

Out of layers of ominous, heated fog, brief outlines of four figures arose. These images had long, black robes with hoods, and they held large crosses with sharp points on the handles. Suddenly, they turned and slowly walked towards me. I just stood there, frozen in my tracks. Soon, the foursome got closer, and they circled around me chanting. Finally, they raised their pointed crosses and started stabbing and killing the figures in front of them, one after another.

I also had the reoccurring dream that my brother, sister, and I were walking through a field towards the house where we first lived. When we walked into the house, we found that it was real quiet. My brother walked in first and laid down on the sofa bed in the living room and covered himself. But there was a person on the couch. Then suddenly, the other person turned over, wrapped his arms around my brother and started killing him. That person was a demon. One could tell that he was being killed by the expression on his face…like he was leaving. His eyes were emptying. My sister and I tried to escape, but we couldn't. I remember having this dream over and over, and each time, I knew what to expect. I tried to warn my siblings about what was going to happen, but they wouldn't listen. And the end result was always the same. We were trapped, and the demons laughed.

Even when I was not asleep, I could often feel a demonic presence. I remember walking along and feeling that people were next to me, but there was no one there. Once I heard "beep, beep, beep", quicker and quicker. Then, I felt something jump on me. I couldn't move. I couldn't scream. I felt that something was completely covering me…like a sense of evil.

I remember that once I was lying on the bed, and my cousin was sitting next to me. I could feel that evil presence coming closer. Then, suddenly, I fell into a paralyzing coma. I couldn't move. It was like my whole body was in a cramp, frozen stiff. In my mind, I was screaming and fighting to move the presence that had absorbed throughout my entire body. But there was nothing I could do. In complete fear, I cried out to God to help me. I continued this prayer over and over until the evil left me. I gasped for air, swinging and kicking, and I screamed a loud, very distorted yell.

I thought that I must have scared my cousin to death, because she jumped off the bed and cried, "What's wrong with you?"

"Why didn't you help me when I needed it?" I yelled. "I was screaming for you to help me. Why didn't you?"

She declared, "No, you were just lying there. You didn't ask for help or scream!"

"Yes, I did! Something was attacking me!" I cried.

Then I explained to her what had happened.

"There is something wrong with you!" she exclaimed.

Then she got up and walked out of the room. I chased after her.

"Don't leave me here by myself," I begged.

Once about 2:00 a.m. when everyone was asleep, I sensed that somebody was outside. I looked out the window and saw that it was a full moon, which allowed me to see down the dirt road and into the field. It seemed like someone was out there, and it was calling me but without words. Afraid of the dark, I opened the door and began to walk down the dirt road. In the next yard, they had huge eucalyptus trees that ran down their property line. With the full moon hitting the corner tree, it looked like the head of Jesus looking at me. I continued to walk in complete fear that wouldn't stop. Something was drawing me towards the field. I turned to look back at the house, and I realized that I was far away from it. I wanted to run back to the house and lock the door, but I was too afraid, expecting that a demonic creature would attack me at any moment. I continued to walk until I realized that I was standing in the middle of the field all alone. I couldn't see them, but I could feel demons all around me. In a paralyzing fear, I thought that if I even breathed, they would attack. I stood still in the field all night until the sun came up and I felt that I was safe. Then, I ran home.

The dreams went on, and so did the bad experiences. But I survived. In fact, throughout my life, things would happen that could not be explained. God had His hand on me and miraculous things would happen all along the way. No doubt someone had been praying for me. Well, there were more than one. Several. And I think my grandfather was one of them. So was my mother.

The Cinder Block House

Driving in the van in search of a new place to live, my mother suddenly spotted a sign on a modest cinder block house that read "For Rent". It was one of three little houses nestled on a little dirt road just down from a quiet street off Highway 4. It was this highway that would some day take me any direction that I wanted to go.

As you entered the small country home, you first came into the kitchen. Then, you would go into the living room. A hallway led to the bathroom, and there were two bedrooms on either side. There was a clearing out in front that would make a great play area, and there were mulberry trees for shade and a big pine tree. It was perfect!

Eager to rent the house, she found the owner and asked if it was still available. He told her that it was but that it was not ready. It was full of garbage and junk and that it needed to be cleaned.. But, that didn't matter to my mother. She knew that we needed a place to stay, so she begged him to rent it to us. She even offered to take it as is.

"I'll clean it up for free!" she exclaimed.

So, she did, and we moved in that same day!

One side of my new street was in Oakley, and the other side was in Knightsen. But as you went farther down the road, it all became the small town of Knightsen. Many residents owned large ranches and farms. Small houses that once housed the workers dotted the streets. Cattle and sheep grazed in separate pastures. Brilliant lemon yellow mustard lined rows of trees in orchards of white and pink, and vibrant green fields of wheat and hay swayed in the soft Delta winds that blew off of the nearby rivers and sloughs. While the neighboring towns carried most of the traffic, Knightsen seemed like a step back into time. It was free from congestion, and everything moved at a slower pace. The main street was (and still is) only a block long. The railroad still runs parallel to the street. There is a post office, a fire station that used to be manned by volunteer firefighters called in by a siren, and a small school that goes up to the eighth grade.

This could have been a description of any place in rural America. But while it may have seemed like an ideal place to grow up as a child, I was so troubled by the effects of abuse, teasing, demons, and my own bad choices that it really didn't make that much difference. I was bound to gravitate towards trouble no matter where I lived.

There were good times when my brothers, sisters, and I used to play in the big clearing near the big pine. There was a short period of time that I experimented with my father's cigarettes. Sometimes when no one was looking, I would steal them, climb up in the tree, and smoke them. I thought I was cool.

I was about six years old, and we were sitting around the house with my family. Suddenly, out of nowhere, my dad would stand up, grab me by the arm, and drag me outside.

Then, he would close the door and yell, "Stay out!"

I guess he was tired of hearing my voice. I knew better than to try to go in, but I was afraid of sitting outside in the dark. Once he went to bed, somebody would open the door and let me in. This happened more than once, but someone would always be there to open the door for me.

One time, I walked into the living room. As usual, my dad was drinking. I noticed that my brothers and sisters were kind of huddled together as if they were taking a family portrait.

I ran up to include myself, but when I got up close, my dad stopped me and said, "You're not my son."

A few days went by, and I made a remark that I had a different dad. He must have heard it, because he grabbed me, dragged me to the back of the house, and started beating me and beating me. I didn't understand why.

Another time, I was riding my bike down the street when a dog began chasing me. He bit my knee. When I looked down and saw the dog, I panicked, started screaming, and riding faster. But the dog hung on to my leg with his teeth, and I dragged it with me. When he finally let go, I rode around the block into the yard and then ran into the house. The sight of all the blood threw me into more of a panic. My dad set his beer down and asked what happened. I was beyond words and continued to scream in fear. He lifted me up into the kitchen sink, ripped off my pant leg, and grabbed a knife.

My mom questioned, "What are you doing?"

He said, as he put the knife to my leg, "I have to cut off his leg to stop the infection."

I began to scream louder trying to escape. But he had a death grip on me holding me down. Suddenly, it didn't seem so bad getting bit by the dog!

My mom was finally able to wrestle me away from my father. As she carried me away, I looked back at my dad as he picked up his beer and continued to drink.

There was an orchard of almond trees next to the house; there was no fence or anything to separate it from the yard.

I remember the rows and rows of trees that seemed to go on forever. It was a perfect place to play. Neighborhood kids would gather in the field after school to play war, tag, or hide and seek.

In March, the trees would be covered in white. Sometimes, I would just sit in the orchard on a breezy day and watch the blossoms float down from the trees like falling snow. I would extend my arms and catch the white petals in my hands like they were gifts from heaven. I loved it there. It was like a fantasy world, and I didn't want to leave. It was there that I could escape from reality.

The tall, green grass between the trees would sway back and forth with the wind like the ocean. I remember running right into the grass and diving into it like I was swimming. Sometimes, I would just lay there and disappear from the world for a while.

But there were times when the field wasn't so pretty any more; it became dark and eerie. Sometimes, it felt like there were people hiding behind or in the trees, only I couldn't see them. Then, in the ominous darkness, I would turn and run away.

Although the kids on the block would play together, most of them were either younger or older, and I never really had any close friends. Other than my brothers and sisters, I was usually alone.

There was a game that the kids in the neighborhood would play. It didn't have a name, but all of a sudden, all the kids would jump on an unsuspecting victim, pin him down, and start grabbing and pulling at him. When it happened to me, I screamed and fought to get loose, but it was useless. Someone's hand would cover my mouth to silence me. No one would have heard me anyway, as Mom was at work, and Dad was busy enjoying his beer. It was just something that happened, so I thought. I didn't really hit me until one day they targeted one of the neighbor boys. When it was over, he picked himself up, screaming with tears coming down his face. He ran away holding his clothes tight to his body. The look on his face as he ran into his house told me that something was really wrong with that game.

I remember walking into the third grade at the new school with high hopes of meeting new friends and to learn. One would think that in a small country school the children would be very nice and accepting. But kids can be cruel anywhere. As I shyly approached the room, I was so shocked. Instead of accepting me, they laughed at me. And it only got worse.

The kids teased me because I was overweight, and I had long, curly, and unruly black hair. I didn't comb it or anything. And when I came to school, the kids would ask me if I was a boy or a girl.

Moreover, in this small country town, most of the children were Anglo, and just a few in the entire school were Hispanic. Sometimes, the kids would go by and call us "Spics" or "Wetbacks".

I was afraid to use the restroom in fear of being in there alone and that demons would come out of unexpected places. There were times when I would just stand at the bathroom door in the school hallway until I couldn't hold it anymore, and I would wet my pants. Then, I would usually take my sweater off and tie it around my waist to hide the accident. But the kids usually caught me and teased me.

My very basic, but well-worn clothes were not as nice as what the other children wore. My pants were torn and raggedy. The uneven cuffs would drag and rip. One of my uncles used to see me, and he would take a scissors to cut off my ragged cuffs so that they wouldn't look so bad. But of course, the others still noticed.

On top of everything else, I didn't know how to behave in the classroom; it seemed that I was always getting in trouble. My sixth grade teacher finally put me in the corner, and I wasn't allowed to turn around or involve myself with the class unless I was spoken to.

The worst was when I was in the fifth through seventh grades and had to ride the bus with high schoolers, as they teased me the most. They would call me names and make fun of me. One girl would blow up her face every time I got on the bus, indicating that I was fat.

Sometimes, I'd argue with them or cuss. But usually I'd just try to ignore them, even though I could hear them talking and laughing about me. Sometimes, I would just put my head down and cry. Then these bullies would be satisfied; they would get the reaction they wanted. And I guess that making a little kid shed tears made them feel better about themselves.

I found myself isolated and alone; it was me against the world. Whatever self- esteem I had left plummeted.

Chapter 2

What? You Look Crazy!

ℵ

One day when I was in the seventh grade, I heard a lot of commotion down the road. As I looked in that direction, I saw a kid about my age that had just moved into the big house on the street. He was acting really wild, and he was hitting somebody and screaming. As it turned out, the boy was beating up his little brother, as I would learn he often did.

I saw something in him that was so much like me that I wanted to become his friend. So I introduced myself to someone I will call "Bill".

It's amazing how kids with great needs and problems are attracted to each other. I think what drew me to Bill the most was that we both pretended that we were in a fantasy world; we were both running from something, but we didn't know what. We became friends right away, and it wasn't long before we were inseparable.

Bill and I used to get into all kinds of trouble…especially at school. Sometimes when we were in the middle of class and everything was quiet, he would suddenly scream, loud, like a girl. He knew that it would make me laugh, and it did! Hysterically! Other times, I would do the screaming, and he would laugh! We were always being sent to the principal's office.

One day, as we walked to catch the bus for school, Bill came out of his house with a long trench coat and a Mohawk.

I remember saying, "What? You look crazy!"

It brought me back to when I was eight or nine when I saw some punk rockers from New York on the Phil Donahue Show. He did an interview with them, and I thought they were cool! I was mesmerized by their look. I saw that they were real angry, and their thrashed clothes, crazy hair, leather jackets, and big boots made a real impression on me. However, I was too young at the time to become like them.

But seeing my friend dressed like this, I knew this was my chance to show my rebelliousness and individuality. I felt I was hated, so I hated others. I asked Bill to show me how to cut my hair that way, and it wasn't long before I, too, had a Mohawk! But it wasn't just any Mohawk; it had brilliant color! Sometimes, it was green and blue. Other times, it was red, orange, and yellow like a flame.

Not really a trusting person, I did not allow anyone else to cut or style my hair. I always shaved my own head, except for the tuft of hair that stood straight up. Then, I would use special hair paint for it. And if I didn't have it, I'd use Jello. A couple of times, I had to use spray paint, and later, I would have to soak my head in hot water to get it out!

I would also wear white and black make-up; my face would be stark white, and my eyes were smeared with black. Sometimes, I would wear red or black lipstick for that corpse look.

As time went by and I got used to my image, I began piercing myself. I stuck safety pins through my shaved eyebrows. For a short time, I had two safety pins that pierced my neck kind of like a tie, and I had a piece of wire that I sharpened with a file that I stuck through the center of my lip. And, of course, I pierced my nose and ears. I would sometimes connect chains to either my eye or my ear or from my nose to my ear. And I sprayed, "I wanted to be hated" on the back of my jacket.

The music I listened to was mostly about world destruction and Satanism. It was hard core punk and speed and death metal. Some of the groups would talk about having sex with the dead, cannibalism, and hatred for God. With my trashy, rebellious attitude, big boots, and wild appearance, I definitely stood out from the rest in the small community.

In a way, I used the crazy punk rocker image to cover up all the pain. I felt that if people were going to hate me, I was going to hate myself more. There seemed to be another person inside of me that no one could understand. That was the weak person who was really me. And then there was a different person who was crazy. And these two people kept battling each other. That wild person was like a shield that protected me.

After a couple of months, Bill took things even further. He started dressing in drag. His outfit included a tight tee shirt tied in the back, skimpy clothes, fishnet stockings, high heels, a long, curly blonde wig, and heavy, heavy make-up. Bill made a very attractive woman, striking, but trashy.

It didn't bother me that he dressed like a drag queen, nor did I put him down for it. We didn't judge each other. We stood by each other. No doubt, we were the least popular kids in school and he was just as messed up as I was, but that didn't matter because we had each other's friendship and we became each other's strength. His insanity and mine were so close that we just bonded. He became my best friend.

One day at school, two guys started to make fun of Bill during recess. I told them to stop teasing him, but they chased him around the buildings. Finally, Bill pulled out a small steak knife and stabbed them. He was arrested and taken to juvenile hall. After he got out, he went to live at a foster home a couple miles away. But nothing changed. We stayed friends, and we would still meet each other, walk to the bus, and hang out together.

When we were the ninth and tenth grades, we would dress in our usual bizarre way and stroll up and down the main highway late at night. One can only imagine how much we stood out in the small country town. Sometimes, we would hang out in front of a local bar, and Bill would flirt with men, acting like he was prostituting. Then, we would laugh. One time, the cops chased us because it was late and, of course, we looked suspicious. When they finally cornered us, they asked us all kinds of questions. Just then, Bill's foster father, who was looking for him, just happened to drive by and pulled over.

"Hey, what's going on?" he inquired. "That's my son."

"Which one?" the policeman asked.

"The one with the wig," the father said. The cops just looked at each other. He looked so much like a girl, they could hardly believe he was his son. He was that convincing.

Sometimes, Bill would dress in his usual female garb and disappear at night. Later on, he'd come back with all sorts of things such as a car, a horse, or whatever he could find. Once he broke into law enforcement officer's ranch and stole some saddles and a horse. Then, he went for a ride!

Another time, he broke into the house next door and stole a record player and all the records.

When I came over to his house, he said, "Let's play D.J."

One of us would play the records, and the other one would dance.

One morning when I was going to the school, Bill and his sister "Laura" picked me up in a shiny red and black MG that they had stolen the night before. I was perched in the back on what wasn't really a seat, and they were in the front. Laura was driving.

Neither one of them knew how to drive a stick, and it was like a comedy to watch them try to figure it out. The car jerked, ground gears, and stalled. At one point, Bill accidentally pulled off the top part of the stick, and they were madly trying to put it back together. I was trying my best to hold on, but I was laughing so hard I almost fell out a couple times. We laughed and yelled as she crazily drove towards school like a trio of clowns. As we turned the wrong way into the parking lot, we were met by a large school bus that was just pulling out of the driveway. The bus swerved wide to miss us, the big tires went up on one side, and it almost tipped over!

The wild clown team dropped me off at school; then, they crashed into someone's yard across the street. After figuring out that they were not hurt, they scattered in different directions.

I went on to class, but that was soon interrupted when I was summoned to the office. It was the deputies. They told me that I was seen in a stolen car, and they started asking all sorts of questions such as "Who was driving?" "Where did we get the car?" "Where did they go?" ... none of which I could answer. I told them that they just picked me up on the road, so the next thing I knew, the deputies let me go.

I usually hung out with Bill's new family. A younger sister was a miracle baby. She was born with Crohns disease and was supposed to die before she was three. But she survived all the way to adulthood.

It was around the same time that I started experimenting with drugs as a young teen. I snorted crank and cocaine. There was a time when I was even younger, maybe nine or ten, when I was with two guys who were smoking a joint. They thought it would be funny to get me high, so they made me sit in front of them and they physically opened my mouth and made me inhale weed. Then, they stared and laughed at me.

Bill's biological sister whom I will call "Tammy" was 6'2", very thin, and as strong as a man. I wouldn't have approached her even if I had a baseball bat. Once, seven guys in Antioch attacked her. She was stabbed in the lung. So she ripped off part of a fence and started swinging. As one of the young men approached her, she jabbed him with the jagged stick. Somehow, he got an immediate bacterial infection and started screaming that his skin was on fire. All of the guys stopped to see what was the matter with their friend. She then had time to reach up to the one that was on top of her and grabbed him in the eye sockets. She had such a strong hold on him that it caused bleeding from his eyes.

"I have never heard anyone scream like that young man!" Tammy exclaimed.

She went to the hospital, and so did he.

Another time, Tammy was in the City Park. She ran over to another girl with whom she was having a problem. Soon, Tammy started beating her up. It didn't bother her that there were policeman nearby, as they were having a picnic with their families at the time. The girl's mother came to rescue her, but she got punched, too. The policeman noticed the fighting and ran over to break it up. They found that she was very hard to handle, and they didn't escape without some injuries. Tammy went to prison for three years for assault on the officers.

Bill's older brother "Peter" was on the wild side. One time, Peter supposedly called the Sheriff's department, claiming that someone was breaking into his house. When they came up to the door, he supposedly ran around the side of the house and jumped into the deputy's vehicle. He drove it around in circles with the siren on. They caught him and put him in a group home.

High School

From fourteen to seventeen, I lived at home, but I mostly hung out on the streets, and sometimes, I went to school.

High school wasn't easy for me. It was a small town then, and the people at the local high school seemed to know each other better. Everyone kind of dressed the same. There were the usual "jocks", cowboys, and cheerleaders. Anyone else was looked down on. There were some rockers and stoners, but they hung out in one little corner of campus. And there were a few punk rockers like me who seemed to appear from different parts of the school district. But sooner or later, they kind of disappeared. Maybe the reason that they didn't last very long was because of the pressure from other kids, or maybe other things. But they were gone.

If you didn't look the same or act the same as the popular groups, you were singled out. Sometimes, you got beaten up or teased. So, most of the kids slowly changed their appearances to blend in with all the rest. But not me.

The school officials made me see a shrink because of the way I dressed and my attitude. My first visit was short.

The doctor said, "I'm going to say a word, and you say the first thing that comes to mind."

"O.k.," I responded.

He said, "Car."

I said, "Hearse."

He stopped and scolded, "If you don't want help, you can go."

So I left.

One day, two guys and I were walking through a crowd of kids. Some of them decided to start pushing us. Some threw rocks, and a couple of them started spitting. I responded by cussing and screaming. I wanted to be hated, but really, I didn't. I guess I was hurt because everyone wanted to fit in and be accepted. But that wasn't what was happening here. I didn't let them know how I felt inside.

I would hang out with Peter and Bill's older sister "Anita" after school. Anita used to come to the high school sometimes, and I would meet her in the park. When she noticed that people stared at me, she responded by standing in their face and verbally shredding them apart. She would tell me when someone says something stupid to punch them in the neck or spit on them. I would laugh, but inside; I didn't feel important enough to defend myself. Peter was more relaxed and didn't let much bother him.

Riding the bus from kindergarten to the eighth grade was hard, but it was harder yet when I was in high school. People would not want me to sit next to them. I was still sporting my Mohawk, and I dressed like a punk rocker. I was different from everyone else, and the kids at school weren't afraid to voice their disapproval. It wasn't uncommon for them to tease me, call me a sissy, and laugh at me. But one day, a couple of guys suddenly grabbed me and threw me to the floor. One of the guys asked if anyone on the bus had a knife or some scissors so that he could cut off my Mohawk. I was humiliated because everybody was looking at me and laughing. One girl soon stood and ran to the back of the bus where all of this was happening.

"Here, I have some scissors!" she exclaimed.

They were those cheap plastic ones, and they weren't able to cut through my thick hair.

I had to fight to keep the tears inside. I remember that one guy stood up and grabbed the scissors out of the other boy's hands and said for him to leave me alone. I was glad that this kid stopped the others, and I knew that I should have thanked him, but I just went back to my seat and sat there motionless until the bus came to my stop. I remember standing up to get off the bus and walking down the isle with everybody laughing and staring at me. I felt like such a fool! But I kept a straight face. I didn't want any of them to know that inside they had just ripped me into pieces. But once I got off the bus, I couldn't hold it back anymore. I remember walking home, and the tears were falling off my face. Thoughts of getting even started to pour through my mind. It wasn't just this incident that I was crying about; it was my whole life. I had developed this extreme hatred for society because of the abuse I had been through and the teasing. I wanted to hate everyone. In my mind, I created this plan to shoot and kill everyone on my street. For this simple feat, I could probably get on t.v. Then, I would be able to get the chance to tell everyone in the world how much I hated them.

Although I could never carry out any of these feelings, nor do I agree with those who do, I felt that I experienced some of the turmoil that campus killers go through due to demonic activity, abuse, teasing, and isolation from other students.

I was truant a lot, and I did not behave in the classroom. I was sent to another school not too far away. Things were about the same as at the other school, but I had some friends at this one. At this school, as well as the last, I would cuss out the teachers in front of class, as I didn't have any respect for teachers or anyone. I hated everyone.

I remember being in class when the teacher walked in and told us that we were going to see a documentary she wanted us to see. It was about teenage runaways and how they survive on the streets. We always welcomed videos because we wouldn't have to do our regular work, but little did I know that this one would be horrifying to me. I had no idea.

I was acting my usual disruptive self when I put my hand at the side of my mouth and loudly whispered, "When I finish high school, I want to be a homeless drug addict!"

"O.k. class. Quiet down! Everyone in your seat!" the teacher demanded.

As the video started, things were cool until it showed people I knew! It was a documentary shot in San Francisco with gay and transvestite prostitutes. I could hardly believe my eyes! I sat there with my mouth wide open in shock! I had gone to San Francisco with Bill and later by myself and hung out with these people on Polk Street! My biggest nightmare was coming true right before my eyes!

"At any moment, my secret could be revealed," I thought. "The camera would show me!"

I didn't know what to do, so I put my head down and expected the worse. That was one of the reasons why I changed my identity. It was a disguise. After all, it was easier to have people hate me for looking like a punk rocker than to hate me because I was gay.

The teacher kept stopping the tape and discussing it. So we really only saw the beginning of it. After class, I told Bill about the tape, and so he slipped into the classroom while the teacher was not there and took it so that nobody could finish watching it.

We violated the rules and in a very rare move that could have gotten me expelled, I did some acid.

At break, I was standing outside, and as I looked down at the ground, I felt that I was slowly falling into darkness. It looked like I was standing on a needle of what was left of the earth. Where the ground was falling had no end. Then, it turned into complete darkness. I finally got up enough courage to tip toe my way back into class. I am not sure how I was able to function the rest of the day. There are many things that I do not recall.

Later, when I arrived home, I tried to avoid my parents, because I knew that if they saw me, they would know I was on something. As I hid in the bathroom, I made the mistake of looking at myself in the mirror. I stared at myself for quite a while. My face started to contort and sway as if it was changing form. Mesmerized by what I was seeing, my face slowly started dripping off. I tired to put my face back together with my hands, but it only seemed to make things worse. Chunks of my face were coming off with every touch. I continued to stare into the mirror, and suddenly I could see my skull inside my head. I closed my eyes, shook my head, and looked again. This happened several times, but I was able to get up the next morning and go to class.

There was one kid whom I had gone to school with for years. One time, he said, "Look what I've got!"

"What is it?" I asked, dying to know.

He pulled out a black book entitled "The Satanic Bible". I was nervous, but also curious. He opened it up, and it said "Open the Gates of Hell", and it had some sort of prayer.

We both read it together (and later, I looked at it even more and took part in some of the rituals). It, no doubt, drew me farther into the dark world of evil.

There was one teacher who always got on me about something. I would argue with her and tell her to leave me alone. She tried to tell me that I was special and that I had the potential to be somebody. I would tell her to "save it" and that I didn't expect to live to see eighteen. I figured that I'd be dead by then. Little did I know that there was so much truth in what she was trying to tell me. But I just continued on the way I always did.

Once I showed her how I had cut myself.

I had a smile on my face when I told her, "Look what I did", and I proudly displayed my carved arm.

She freaked, grabbed my arm, and walked me to the office. I asked her where we were going.

"I'm going to call the police," she replied.

"Why?" I asked.

She said that it was against the law to cut oneself...something about self-mutilation. I was able to calm her down so that she wouldn't call the police.

Soon after, another kid and I were able to make a joke out of it. We got the little pins that go into the bulletin board, and we stuck four or five of them through the eraser at the tip of a pencil.

Next, we swung the pencil so that the pins would hit our arms and say, "Look, teacher, self mutilation", then laugh.

Even though neither one of us played an instrument, another student and I would sit in class and dream about being in a hardcore trash band. If our fantasy had come true, we would have sung songs about hating society, lawlessness, and Satanism. The name of our band would have been called "Death by Suicide."

When talking to the principal later on, I asked how I was in school. He replied, "You mean like the time you cussed me out in front of the student body?"

And for that, he expelled me (as well he should have).

Karen

I met a young lady whom I will call "Karen" at the park. She was going out with a guy I knew, and they were always together. They were all into the rocker lifestyle. The guy did tattoos, and she was like his groupie. In fact, they made a really good couple. So, it was kind a strange when she came up and started talking to me when I was sitting in the park.

"Where's your boyfriend?" I asked.

Karen quickly changed the subject. We started talking, and we found out that we got along really well. So we started to hang out. The more that we were together, the more her appearance started to change. She went from tennis shoes and no make-up to combat boots and black make-up like mine. She even went so far as to let me cut her long blonde hair, shave her head, and fashion what remained into a fifteen inch Mohawk. Then, I dyed it apple green. It was crazy!

One day, we were walking down the street, and a guy made a comment.

"You guys make a good couple," he remarked.

That is when it hit me that she liked me. I wasn't mentally prepared for this to happen. In fact, it caught me off guard. From that point on, everywhere we went, I made sure that there was somebody with us. She tried hinting to me that she wanted to be with me, but I would blow it off. But the more I did, the more it seemed like she wanted to be with me. She started buying me drugs, tried to get me to drink, and she gave me money. And it became harder and harder to avoid the situation. I liked her, but just not in the way that she wanted me to. I wasn't ready or able to explain to her why.

The strange thing was that one of the reasons why I dressed the way I did was because I thought that nobody would like me. There were not many punk rockers in the little town I lived in. Karen and everybody just thought I was a weirdo.

One day, Karen came to my house, and she brought her stepbrother with her. He looked very familiar, but I couldn't put my finger on where I had seen him before. Then, a few weeks later, I was in San Francisco with Bill, and there was Karen's stepbrother standing on the corner on Polk Street, where young gay guys would come to prostitute. We walked past each other, but we didn't speak. But in my mind, I knew that he was going to tell Karen. That was a part of my life that I wanted to keep a secret. A few days later, I talked to Karen, and she told me that her stepbrother told her everything. But I just denied it all, and she believed me.

That night, Karen wanted to party with just me. I told her that I would let her know, but I never got back to her. After that, we didn't talk for a while. After a few months, I went to her house to see how she was doing. I really liked Karen, and I wanted to be her friend. Just not her boyfriend. So, I went to her house, and we started talking.

She asked, "Remember that day we were supposed to get together and you never got back to me?"

I said, "Yes".

"Well", she responded. "That night I ended up going to a party, and I got drunk out of anger. Then, I slept with some guy and got pregnant."

That was the last time I saw Karen. I thought about her over the years. I thought that if things could have been different, I would have married Karen, had a family, and had a normal life. She proved in many ways that she wanted to love me. The problem was that I didn't know how to love her back.

With everything that I was going through in school and all my secrets I had inside, I began to lash out at others. I was angry, and I need to vent. And I took it out on my poor mother. Mom would be in the kitchen washing dishes, and I would be sitting behind her at the kitchen table. I would tell her how much I hated her and that I hated my dad just as much. I was really out of control. I cussed at her and told her that I hoped she and my dad would die. I remember her just looking back at me.

Originally, I wanted to tell my mother everything that was going on in my distorted life, but I was ashamed to tell her that nobody at school liked me and that I was being harassed every day. So I just started screaming at her. I told her that I was going to kill myself and that when I died, I would take her and Dad to hell with me. I can still see her face. It was almost as if she was in shock. She tried to tell me to be quiet, but I kept talking louder and louder until I was yelling. I remember telling her that my father had raped me when I was a child. She looked at me in disbelief and told me to get out of their house. She kept screaming at me to get out. I walked out of the front door and into the middle of the road.

But soon after, I asked myself, "Where can I go now?" as I stood in the middle of the street turning in circles.

It was a good thing for the shed.

Back to the Shed.

My grandmother moved out of her house in Oakley, and my parents took over the mortgage and moved in. I was in the house for a while, but they always kept kicking me out. So, I'd go out to the shed where we used to live years before. That is where I kept my things anyway, and it was easier for me to live out there. Out there, I could get away and be myself.

But I wasn't always alone. I could feel an evil presence out there. Demons would appear in the room with me, and sometimes, they would be outside. There was one time that I walked into the shed, and there was a distorted figure vibrating wildly and out of control. My door didn't have a doorknob, and when I went to open it, I noticed an eye looking in. The eye was bigger than the hole in the wall, and I thought that if the eye is that big, what would the body look like? Once I got up the courage, I kicked the door open, only to see what looked like laundry hanging over the fence that went around the yard. But instead of clothes, it was like human flesh hanging over the fence with the skeletons ripped out.

At night, I kept hearing someone walking on the roof, scratching at the window, and rattling the door as if someone was trying to break in. And this was when there was no wind. So, I would get up out of bed and go look around. I looked for footprints around the window and door, but I found nothing. I tried to find a reasonable explanation for these things, but I couldn't. So, I spray painted the window black and boarded it up with pieces of wood. I chained the door closed and sometimes, I would nail it shut from the inside. But I could still sense that there were demons there.

I really thought that it was the neighbor who was doing all this. He was under suspicion for having shot his wife two times in the head but was not charged with the murder due to lack of evidence. I imagined that he climbed the fence over to our yard because the top of the wire fence was bent inward towards me. But again, there were no footprints.

Our house, if not entire neighborhood, seemed to be surrounded by death. In addition to the murder of the housewife, there was another neighbor who walked with his seven-year-old daughter down to the end of the street, shot and killed her, and then turned the gun on himself. And just one house and a field over was where my brother was murdered.

I couldn't walk between the shed and the house if it got too dark, because it was too scary. The demons had traumatized me, and I was paralyzed with fear. If I stayed out there too late, I couldn't go to the house because I was afraid of what would happen to me out in the dark. My paranoia trapped me in the shed night after night.

CCC

Some time went by since I had been expelled from school, and I wasn't doing anything with my life. I was tired of being nagged to get a job, so I decided to join the California Conservation Corps. I was surprised that they accepted me!

The present day CCC programs are national, state, and local organizations that involve young people in community service, training, and educational activities. I seemed to thrive in such an atmosphere. Believe it or not, it was probably the first time in my life that I had ever done anything positive. It didn't take me long to get used to the activities, wear a uniform, and follow the rules.

My supervisor was real cool. He never looked down on me for being punk rock. In fact, he always talked about his girlfriend from England who was punk rocker, too. He basically took me under his wing and taught me all the skills I needed. And just like the teacher in continuation school, he told me that I could be anything I wanted to be. I was just as important as anyone else. I soaked up the attention like a sponge, and in return, I tried my hardest to be the best worker possible. My self-esteem shot up to an all time high, and it didn't take long before I got promoted to crew leader in charge of sixteen.

I was sent to San Luis Obispo for two weeks for leadership training, and I came back as a leader to a crew in Pittsburg. I trained with CAL-OSHA and CALTRANS. I was able to work on environmental projects and best of all, with state emergency programs. We went in when there were floods, earthquakes, and fires.

I was able to go on two fires. The first one was in Los Angeles County, and we were there for four days. We worked long hours, night and day. We were right next to the firefighters, volunteers, and the prison crews. It was definitely a learning experience in doing something positive, and I was proud of myself; I was doing something important. I was able to see things that I had never seen in my life, and I did things that I never imagined doing. Some of the guys weren't able to handle the job, and they quit. So we were always getting new people. But I wanted to stay. To me, it was exciting.

The second fire that we went on was in Ventura County in Southern California. We were there for a few days. This time, our supervisor was called away for a few days, and we got a substitute. Being the crew leader, my job was to make this man's job as easy as possible. But from the moment I met him, I knew that there were going to be problems. He was careless, and he tried to shortcut around everything. Instead of helping to get our campsite up, the new boss sloughed off and went over to talk to the other supervisors from different crews. Our crew set up camp. Later on that night, the big brass, the leaders of the Conservation Corps walked up to both of us.

One of the VIPs introduced himself and then addressed the sub.

"You know, if you watch this guy for a while, you might learn how to do your job better!" the leader said.

The substitute looked at me with a stone-cold, angry stare. He was thoroughly embarrassed. We were both shocked to hear that come out of the leader's mouth. Slowly, I turned and walked away, trying to act like that didn't just happen.

We did our job for the next few days, then we were dismissed to go home. Everyone was tired, and it was a long ride. Upon reflecting on this assignment, I realized that one thing about these trips is that you learn how to work with people, whether or not you like them. You create a bond with the guys on your crew because you have worked together to do something positive. The new boss was the last thing on my mind, as I was tired and glad to be back. My ride had just arrived, so I picked up my bags, and I said good-bye to everyone. I started to leave when he called me back and said that he wanted to talk to me in private. I said O.K., put my bags down, and walked into the office.

The substitute super was filling out a paper, and he said, "Sign here."

Automatically, I began to sign, but in the middle of my signature, I asked, "What is this?"

He responded, "Your termination papers. You're fired! You will never make a fool out of me again!"

I was speechless and shocked, but I continued to sign. Then, I walked out of the room, picked up my bags, and walked down to the parking lot, ignoring all the guys who were saying good-bye. When I got to the car, this overwhelming feeling of pain came over me, and my eyes began to tear up. I felt like something had been ripped right out of me. Everything that I had accomplished in the last sixteen months was right out the window because of someone else's insecurities. Whatever self-esteem I was able to build and every positive thing that had come out of the CCC were gone. How could I have been such a fool to believe that this would be different than anything else I had ever experienced in my life? I completely let down all my walls, and I trusted for the first time. But everything was taken away, and once again, I was left with very low self-esteem and distrust. I remember telling myself that I would never put myself in that position again where someone could lie and betray me that way. I was destroyed.

A few weeks went by, and I just sat around the house. I didn't want any part of the world, for in my eyes, it was a bad place. One day, a friend came by, and I started to talk to him outside. He explained to me that he was selling drugs and because we had gotten high together in the past, he wondered if I wanted to help him. I realized that this would be a way to stay high without paying for it, or so I thought.

I said, "Okay," and he left me with a bag and said that he would be back in a couple of days to pick up the money and to bring some more.

I went into the shed and started smoking, and all of a sudden, life was bearable again.

More About My Family and Extended Family

Once, I was walking down the street and around the corner where a family friend lived. The man grew up with my father. As I approached the house, I noticed an old Mazda truck with a shell. As I walked closer, the back of the truck opened, and two men came out. One of them was my father. Before I could ask him what he was doing, a woman climbed out, pulling on her shirt. By the looks on their faces, I could tell they were all up to no good. The woman tried to talk to me, but I just ignored her. She didn't matter to me. I could tell that my father was wasted by the drunken smile on his face and the beer in his hand.

He tried to tell me not to tell my mother, but I declared, "No one cares what you do."

Whenever he wanted to pull rank on me, he would change personalities and act like a drill sergeant. He would tell me to stand at attention. Then he would yell at me and tell me to do fifty push-ups.

When he gave me such orders, I just laughed at him and said, "You're crazy. I'm not a soldier. I hate this country."

To change the subject, I pulled out a bag of crank and asked him if he wanted to get high.

"Dad, come on. Let's go to the side of the house and smoke it."

I let him "hit the foil" twice, then I told him that it cost $20. I figured that if he was going to throw his money away, he might as well buy some drugs from me.

Needless to say, I didn't have a good relationship with my father. Nor were things any better with my brothers. My oldest brother was like a steel wall, and he wouldn't talk to me at all.

My other brother was usually mean to me most of my life. When I was sixteen, he would walk into my room and punch me in the throat or kick me in the stomach. Then, he would laugh. One time, I walked into the hallway, and he came from the other direction. As he passed, he grabbed me by the throat and dragged me around. I noticed that there just happened to be a handsaw lying on the floor. During the commotion, I was able to pick it up and I put it to his throat.

At the same time, I screamed," I hate you, and I'm going to cut your head off!"

He looked at me with that frozen stare I had often seen in his eyes. Then, he released me from the hold, stood up, and laughed.

Even though we all lived in the same house, we could have all been strangers. My brother was very quiet, and he kept to himself. We never really talked. I knew that he was an addict, but it was as if we were on two different planets. We were that far apart.

Sometime later, I was hanging out down the street when I noticed that Mom's car kept going up and down the road. At first, it didn't seem strange, but after she kept driving back and forth, it became quite noticeable.

When she saw me, she stopped and with a panicked look on her face, she yelled, "Have you seen your brother?"

Before I could answer her, she cried, "Something is wrong. I can feel it. I haven't seen your brother for a couple of days!"

One night, not long after my mother drove around looking for him, I was sitting at the kitchen table. My mother, who was sitting in the living room, began to talk about him and how something just wasn't right.

"Why hasn't he come home? He always comes home to eat something," she asked with fear in her voice.

I rudely interrupted her by saying, "Who cares about my brother? I hate him!"

She yelled at me to shut my mouth, but that just made me angrier.

I said, "I hope that they find him dead in a ditch!"

Just as I finished my sentence, a car drove up the road. You could tell by the glare in the window and the way that the lights lit up the living room that whoever it was had parked outside. We watched the silhouettes of unknown men in dark suits walk into the yard and up to the door. My mom, being the closest to the front of the house, went to the door. The men showed their badges and told her that they were detectives. They then showed my mother a picture and asked if she knew who it was.

It was my older sister!

My mother replied, "Yes, that's my daughter!"

The officers went on to explain that they had found the picture in a wallet that was in a pocket of a body that someone discovered in the field. They explained that the body had been in there for seven days. They didn't know how the person was murdered, because it was bloated and it began to rip apart. They told her that they had no choice but to cremate it.

My mother cried in disbelief, but at the same time, I guess she knew that my brother was gone. It was her worst nightmare come true.

It wasn't long after that she slipped into a depression that lasted many years.

Although my mother never saw his body, she couldn't or wouldn't admit that the person that they had found was her son. She went through the motions of the funeral and all that, but in her mind, she wanted to believe that he was still alive.

After the funeral, she often stood by the door, just staring in the direction of the dirt road. I would watch her and wonder what she was thinking.

As she opened the door, she put one foot outside, called his name and cried, "It's okay now. You can come home. Nobody's going to hurt you. Just come home!"

According to the detectives, my brother and two friends broke into a towing yard on the Highway 4 in Oakley. They were stealing parts so that they could sell them. As they were leaving, my brother got into an argument with one of the young men he was with. The other robber started to speak louder and louder, so my brother told him to be quiet, repeatedly. The guy must have gotten agitated or nervous, because he turned on him and shot him four times in the face, killing him. He then left his body out in a lonely field not that far from home.

The place where my brother was murdered was the same field that I had nightmares about growing up. It was the nightmare where I walked out of the field and into the house where my brother was laying down on a couch, a demon attacked him, and he died.

I was sixteen at the time, and I had so much hate in me that I hated myself, I hated my family, and I hated God. I remember that I couldn't cry about my brother's death.

I announced to my mom, "I'm glad he is dead! When he was alive, he used to beat me up all the time."

Although I had said that I hated my brother, I really felt bad after his death.

They offered counseling to my family. At first, I really didn't talk about him, but I began to tell the counselor how miserable I was. After hearing some of the things I said, he asked to talk to my mother. He told her that he wanted to put me on some medication but that he couldn't because of my age.

I never knew why my brother had so much animosity towards me until many years later. My sister told me that while growing up, I was the only kid who dressed like a punk rocker in our town and that all others made fun of me. Sometimes, both he and my sister would fight with other teenagers at school or around town in my defense. And at the same time, they would be angry at me for being such an embarrassment to them. I didn't realize that he did care for me, even though he was angry most of the time. He cared or maybe even loved me enough to defend me at school.

After a thorough police investigation, the shooter and the other robber were apprehended. The murderer was eighteen, but since he was only seventeen at the time the crime was committed, he was not tried as an adult and was put into juvenile hall and released in seven years.

Now, after all these years, and although the builders don't know anything about my brother, it seems fitting that they are building a church on the site where the young man who used to see angels died.

My extended family was also plagued or cursed with all sorts of evil. My cousins on my mothers' side were into drugs and gangs, while my paternal cousins were involved with incest, murder, and rape. Some were insane. Many of them went to prison. I had a cousin from my father's side who shot at another cousin, because he had eaten his hamburger.

One of my cousins broke into a shop. When met by the owner, this cousin shot and killed him. Then, he saw the shopkeeper's wife, and he raped her. He went to prison.

When I was twelve or so, another paternal cousin put a knife to my throat and asked if I wanted to know how it felt to bleed to death. He then asked my sister to go ask the neighbor lady to come out so that he could rape her.

This was a normal conversation for him. That's how he was. Everyone was afraid of him, even his own parents, because he would kind of "snap!"

Another cousin got in trouble with some people, and they shot him up with battery acid. By the time he got to the hospital, he was burning from the inside and his teeth were falling out.

Still another cousin was found dead in the desert wrapped in barbed wire from head to toe.

Chapter 3

Downward Spiral

ᘓᘐ

There were times when I would ditch school, and I'd disappear for a couple weeks at a time.

Bill knew about a place on Polk Street in San Francisco where runaway homosexuals prostituted. I would go with him there, often in a car that he had stolen. That became our new hangout. It was a strange situation, because we lived in a small town and while there, we had to act a certain way (well, we were supposed to behave a certain way), but when we went to the city, we could do and be whatever we wanted.

Watching all the other guys prostitute, getting in and out of cars, and talking about it afterwards made me want to do that, too. I longed to be wanted by somebody, but inside I felt ugly, and I wouldn't even try. Although I did not prostitute myself until later when I was heavy into drugs, I envied them. I thought they felt they were needed. I wanted to feel needed, too. That is how lonely I was. So, I continued to hide myself behind the punk rock persona to cover up my pain. I hated myself, I would tell people off, and I wanted people to think I didn't care. I wasn't willing to admit to myself that I was gay.

I remember that the first time I got high, I was hooked! I was fourteen, and I told myself that if getting high feels like this, I don't ever want to come down. Before I knew it, I had a serious addiction. Drugs became my life and an escape route for me.

One thing that I used to say was "Kill me, or get me high!" "Dope or death!"

One time when I was fifteen, I caught the Bart in Concord to San Francisco. I sat down in the little seat that had one seat facing it near the front. The train was almost empty, but a man got on in Berkeley and instead of taking one of the many regular available places, he sat down in that little seat across from me. He looked like Colonel Saunders, but he was all in white. He had long white hair, a white goatee, white, white skin, and he was dressed in a white suit, white shoes, and white hat.

The man began talking to me, telling me things about myself that no one else knew. It really threw me off.

As he stood up at his stop, he looked at me one last time and calmly said, "If I told you where I came from, you wouldn't believe me. But I want to tell you that everything is going to be all right."

After that, my life spiraled downward fast. Things just seemed to spin out of control. However, I kept remembering the man in white. Could he have been an angel, a messenger from God?

I remember it was Halloween, and some friends and I decided to go into the city. When we got to Berkeley, a friend and I got off the train. We agreed to meet up with some other friends later. When we got to her house, we smoked a bunch of crack. Then, at the last minute, she decided to stay home. So I made my way to the city by myself. As I sat there on the Bart at the station, I noticed my friends in a train on the other side of the tracks going the opposite direction. I had no choice but to continue my trip to the city. When I got there, I went to the usual hang out. The city was crowded, and there was a lot of partying going on.

I was standing in front of a porn shop when a man asked me, “What are you doing here all by yourself?”

I told him that I was stranded, and I was trying to catch the train back home. After talking for a while, he invited me into the store and took me into the back where they had little two-person rooms where you could watch X- rated movies. We sat down, and he played a movie. Then, he began to make moves on me. He leaned over and told me what he wanted to do to me. I looked at him in a confused way. He looked at me and just stopped. We walked back outside, and he asked how much a ticket cost back to my house. I told him $4.00, and he gave it to me. I thanked him and walked to the Bart station. I waited for the rest of the night for it to open. And the next day, I went home. I was spared from an evil situation.

Finally, I was able to connect with the other kids on the streets. We were like one big family. Sometimes, Bill, some guys, and I would all go hang out at the park in the city. It was kind of like everybody was taking a break in the middle of the night. Some were playing tag, some were swinging, and some were just talking, laughing and having a good time. Some of the guys were so convincing that you could be hanging out with them all dressed in drag and completely forget that they were boys until they pulled off their wigs or spoke in a deep masculine voice, and everybody would laugh. But as I looked around, I realized that it wasn’t about fun and games. Every one of these guys belonged somewhere or to someone. They were somebody’s child or somebody’s brother, and for some reason, they wound up there. What goes on in a person’s life to get them to the point that they have to live on the streets and sell themselves to survive?

One night, a guy approached a friend of mine.

I didn’t know what happened, but I remember him saying, “Come on.”

So I followed my friend into the alley.

He cried, "Look what the man gave me."

They were cigarettes that had crack in them. So we started smoking one after the other. The alley was dark and dirty, and it had a strong stench of urine and feces. There were people walking back and forth, but I didn't care. We continued to smoke.

I laughed and said, "I want to be a crack head!"

The streets were always crowded, and there was always something going on. People were often engaged in fighting, dealing, and hooking. One day, a man brushed past me, pushing my shoulder. As I turned to look, I heard yelling, then a "pop". At first, I didn't know what it was. The crowd went crazy! People started running in all different directions, hiding behind cars and trying to escape. The popping noise was a single bullet that hit that man in the side of the head.

As he lay there motionless on the ground, he screamed "Help," "Help."

Blood began to form underneath him. The man was less than an arm's distance away from me when he got hit. Someone called 911, and the ambulance took him away. Afterwards, the crowd gathered to talk about it. To me, it was more exciting than scary. I don't know what happened to the man.

I remember there was a kid standing by a pay phone telling us it was his birthday. You could tell he had been drinking because of the slur in his voice, and you could smell the liquor. He was telling us that he wanted to talk to his mom. As he picked up the phone, he asked to be connected to his mother. Apparently, there was no connection, because he started screaming at the operator, telling him or her that all he wanted to do was to talk to his mom on his birthday.

"Please," he cried. "Please let me talk to her."

As I watched him, I realized that he didn't have any idea how to get a hold of her. He began jumping up and down and slamming the phone on the wall. He cursed and screamed and then threw himself on the ground. A couple of us stood next to him while he cried and tried to grab the sidewalk. The others just looked down or rushed to get away from him. But I stayed. This young man, as well as many others living on the streets, did not have a home to go to at night like I did. I had so much more in comparison. Yet, by watching him made me realize how empty life can be and how lonely I was. The loneliness of this lifestyle was overwhelming. At the time, I didn't know that there was a God who could take that emptiness and lonely feeling away.

My home might not have been the best place in the world, but compared to some of the guys, I guess my situation wasn't so bad. Some of these young men were abandoned and disowned, and they lived an everyday struggle of addiction, prostitution, and HIV.

There are a lot of kids out there on the streets. They may have the appearance that everything is o.k. and that they are happy in what they are doing, but they're not. They're lost.

First Suicide Attempt

Bill went to live with his boyfriend in San Francisco, but I still liked to hang out with his family. When I was nineteen, I became friends with a sixteen year old young man who had been placed in their foster home. I am sure that this young man saw me as an older brother, but in my twisted mind, I wanted to believe something else. I thought that I was falling in love with him. My definition of love was selfishness and the same kind of perversion that I was taught as a child. I didn't know any different. I got so frustrated that I didn't know what to do about it. I didn't like myself. That probably stemmed from all my childhood abuse. I slipped into a deep depression.

"I didn't want to be a homosexual, but why was I thinking those thoughts?" I wondered.

I was never able to admit to myself that I was gay. I tried to hide behind the punk rock person I had created.

I didn't know how to deal with my feelings, and the confusion became overwhelming. All of my life I was battling an identity crisis. I could do one of two things. I could try to make a move on this kid and continue the abusive pattern I was taught, or I could pretend like everything was normal. The battle became too much and overwhelming, and I decided that I would be better off killing myself. There was just no way I could continue on this way.

So, I found a bottle of seventeen prescription pills and swallowed them. They were either painkillers or downers. All that I remember after that was that everything turned gray.

My aunt had seen me on my way to the shed.

She told my mother, "I saw him walk by the window, but it's so quiet out there and dark."

I was lying on the bed crying.

My mother came in and asked, "What's wrong?"

"I don't want to live anymore," I yelled.

She asked why. I said that I didn't know; I just didn't want to live any more. She didn't know anything. No one did, except God.

My mother and my aunt took me to the ER. I was barely awake. I kept going in and out of consciousness. Usually people didn't take me serious, even the psychiatrist from before. They would just take one look at me and would think that I was just playing games. However, the doctor did ask what I took. The cloud that was sitting on my memory lifted a little, and I told him that I didn't know exactly but that I just took a bottle of pills.

He asked what I was trying to do. I said that I was trying to kill myself. He asked why I wanted to die. I told him that

I was just tired of being alive.He said that there was nothing that they could do for me, so they sent me to the county mental facility in Martinez.

Actually, I was happy to be there. For some reason, I thought that it would a good thing to be in a straight jacket in a rubber room. It was a safe place, yet I still defended myself with a "smart mouth" attitude.

One of the inmates at the facility tried to intimidate me.

He called to me, "Come here, come here! I want to show you something. The Devil lives under my bed."

He was trying to scare me, but showing no fear I casually replied, "He does? Then who lives in my closet?" That shut him up.

It was then that I heard a small, still voice somewhere inside saying, "Why are you in such a hurry to end your life? Don't you know that you will go to a worse place and that it will be forever?"

At the time, I didn't know where that come from, but now I know that it was from God and that His words had a great impact on me.

The counselor who talked to me when I was in high school wasn't able to help me with my mental illness, and the County wasn't able to offer assistance either. After two weeks in the mental ward, they just let me out. Nothing was solved. Nothing was different. I still didn't know who I was, and I couldn't wait to get high.

The Basement

I was living on the streets and in abandoned houses and cars. I would also bounce from place to place, and sometimes I would get comfortable somewhere. At one time, I stayed at a lady's house, and we would party day and night. She had a normal job, and while she was at work, I would just kick back in the house. She had a sister who lived with her, and her brother often came from out of town to hang out with us, too. But that only lasted for so long. She soon decided to move in with a friend from out of town. I remember the day that she left. We all helped her pack up and drive off.

As we stood there, a friend asked, "Where will you go now?" That was a profound question, as I was later to learn.

"I don't know," I said.

"Well, you are welcome to live at our house," he replied.

He was talking about living with himself, his wife, and two kids at his place in Vallejo.

I replied, "O.k., let's go."

And so, I moved in with my friends.

I was smoking a lot of crank at the time, but it didn't seem like it was ever enough. I snorted quarter lines, smoked grams at a time, and I was even eating it in "bombs", which was either wrapped in toilet paper and swallowed like a pill or in the empty shell of a pill capsule. But it never satisfied, and I always wanted more. I noticed that my friend who owned the house would "slam dope" (shoot it up), and I was curious. I asked what it was like.

"Don't ever try it," he warned. "If you do, you won't ever be able to stop."

My brother used to slam dope before he was murdered. Somewhere in my mind, I thought that because he did that and was killed at an early age, maybe it would be a way to end my life without doing it myself. I didn't know that I was searching for something, and I didn't know what.

I asked my friend to shoot me up, but he said "no" and to never ask him again. I thought that he would agree to inject me because I was holding a bag of crank that he could have had as payment. But I was wrong. He still refused. After a few days, we were partying at his house. I kept bugging him to teach me how to shoot up. Finally after days of begging, he gave in and said, "All right".

But he also declared, "I don't want to be responsible for what could happen to you the rest of your life."

"Are you sure you want to do this?" he questioned again.

I rolled up my sleeve, stuck out my arm, and said, "Hit it!"

I had no idea what was in store for me. Part of me was scared. Part of me just didn't care, but I was also excited and waited impatiently.

I asked myself, "Am I going to get too high? Am I going to be able to handle it? Will something go wrong? Will I be taking too much and die?"

All of these thoughts and worries raced through my mind, but none of them affected me enough to change my mind. He stuck the needle in my vein. I closed my eyes, and he continued to talk to me.

Then he said, "There, I'm done."

As I opened my eyes, I could feel the shot flow through my body. My head got heavy. I lost my breath for a few seconds, and my vision became blurry. So, I sat down for a few minutes until I was able to grab reality. But my life would never be the same. There was no turning back at that point. That was the day that I fell into the arms of Satan. I felt that throughout my entire existence on earth, he had been chipping away at my life, taking it piece by piece. But that day, he had all of me.

I remember walking out of the basement a few hours later, dazed, smiling, and higher that I had ever been. It was like all the years of pain and feelings of darkness and hopelessness were gone in one little shot. I remember thinking that I would never come down, but I soon learned otherwise. I remember being so high that I thought I was Superman. The down side to that was that reality was my "kryptonite." I found that in order to stay in that euphoric state, I had to have more. Later that night, I went back into the basement with my friend for another fix. And that was the last thing I remembered.

My friend's wife told me that I was in the basement for about a week and a half. But the only thing that I remember was that the bag of crank that I was going to bribe him with was gone. I also recalled asking her how I got in the basement and what direction I needed to go to get home. I was in Vallejo, and my home was some 50 miles away in Oakley… or wherever I could find to stay.

The only thing that I could think about was getting high again. At the time, my friend's truck was broken down, and as he fixed it, I waited patiently. But what was supposed to be a few hours turned into a few days.

He asked, "Why do you want to go back to that area anyway? There's nothing out there for you."

I answered, "D (drugs)! Maybe you have other reasons to want to live, but I don't."

And he went back to work on his truck. I went across the street, sat on the sidewalk, and began to see the reality that the drugs were gone. I was coming down in a bad way. It felt like my skin was crawling and that I was suffocating. Time was running out. If I didn't do something quick, there was no telling what would happen.

So I started walking and walking. Next thing I knew, I came to the freeway. I went up an onramp and continued along the emergency lane as the cars sped by on my side. That was about 9:00 p.m., I was tired, but I kept on going. All I could think about was getting another bag, because I didn't want to come down. But after walking all night, the drugs wore off even more.

Soon, the sun came up. I didn't really know where I was; nothing looked familiar to me. I knew that if I just kept going, I would have to end up some place. That was the way my life was. I was headed somewhere, but I didn't know where.

I looked back in exhaustion and remembered the long night on the freeway. I thought about turning around, but it was too far. Just then, a highway patrol officer slowed down and stopped.

When I first saw him, I thought, "Oh, good. He will give me a ride to where I want to go."

But he just got out of his vehicle and asked, "What are you doing?"

I told him that I was trying to get back to Oakley.

"So where's your car?" he questioned.

"I don't have one. That's why I am walking," I answered.

He searched me and told me that it was against the law to walk on the side of freeway.

"Get off at the next off ramp!" he insisted.

"And do what?" I asked.

He may have thought that I was being a smart mouth and really didn't show much respect for someone who was just interested in my safety. But actually, I was confused and really didn't know what to do.

He said that I should call someone to come and pick me up. I told him that I didn't know anyone who would do that.

"How did you get out here anyway?" he asked.

I said that I was at a party and that I got left behind.

As he turned away from me and got back in his car, he demanded, "Get off the freeway. If I see you again, I'll take you to jail!"

And he drove off.

Disregarding his warning, I continued to walk on the freeway for a few more hours. I finally got to the Benecia Bridge, which is a part of a major highway spanning the Cartinez Straits. Suddenly, I spotted an emergency telephone.

"Ah, at last, I'll be rescued," I thought with a great sense of relief.

I picked up the phone with great expectations and spoke to the operator. I told her that I was stranded and that I needed to get across the bridge. She said that someone would be there to assist me soon. I was really glad that help was finally coming, that I could get across the busy bridge, and get home. I knew that every step was a step closer to the next high!

But guess who pulled up?

The same cop!

When I saw him, I turned and started moving away.

But he drove closer, motioned, and sternly said, "Come here."

I knew I was in trouble.

"O.k. Now you're going to jail!" he exclaimed.

I tried to argue with him, but there was nothing that I could say to persuade him to let me go. He kept saying that the freeway was made for driving a car.

"I know," I replied.

I don't know if he felt sorry for me or if he had something else he had to do, but he said, "I'm not going to take you to jail, but you see that off ramp? Get off and follow the road along the side of the freeway, and it will take you back to Vallejo."

"Vallejo? That is where I started from!" I thought to myself, knowing better than to say that to the officer.

I wanted to go in the opposite direction. To Oakley! But I had no choice. So, I went down an off ramp and turned back on an unfamiliar street. By this time, I had been walking for about fourteen hours. I was tired and coming down so hard from drugs made me confused and disorientated. I knew that I was lost, and everything seemed like it was a million miles away. But I continued on. The more the drugs wore off, the more the pain that I was running away from in the first place came alive inside of me. The pain got so bad that I began to weep. I felt hopeless.

I saw an overpass that would take me over and across the freeway. There was a cyclone fence on both sides of it. I walked out onto the middle of the bridge and just stood there watching the traffic below.

I tried so hard to climb the fence, because I wanted to throw myself into the traffic. It seemed like the only sensible thing to do. I remember my fingers frantically grasping the metal strands of the fence as I was trying to convince myself to climb over. But I just couldn't. I'm not sure why.

After about two hours of fighting with myself, I ran off the overpass, threw myself on the ground, and started screaming. I was completely broken and desperate. It was like I wanted to die so bad, but I wasn't able to cause my own death. I was even a failure at that! I failed at everything else, and after that day, I was able to put suicide on the list.

It was my first experience with shooting up, and it didn't help me at all. And here I thought it was going to be so great. Instead, it brought me down even lower than I was before. I felt that I was at the lowest level of existence. And that was all I was doing: existing… but not well.

I remember hearing two little kids talking about me, asking, "Hey, what's wrong with that man? Why is he crying?"

But when I lifted up my head and stood up, there was no one there! I mean there were no people, no houses, nothing! Just trees and hills.

I have often wondered if they were angels who were showing love and concern for me… of all people. Did they reflect God's love for a human being who was completely broken and could not have sunken further down in life?

In my attempt to figure out where the voices came from, I completely forgot about everything that had happened to me in the basement and on the freeway, and soon I made my way back to Vallejo and eventually, Oakley.

Harley

Once, I stayed in a car in a trailer court in Knightsen. The car belonged to a man I will rename "Harley", one of my drug buddies. Harley was quite a character. He was a short, little man who had a long mustache and beard. He didn't have any teeth, and he had wild, brown, stringy hair that grew down past his shoulders and stuck out in all directions. He looked like he had been rolling around in the dirt for a couple of years! He probably only took a bath once a month, and, no doubt, that was also the only time he combed his hair. He used to tell people that he was a troll and that he was born under a bridge.

Sometimes, he came out of his trailer with those trick glasses that had eyes that fell out on springs. He looked so funny with his eye hanging out and his wild hair!

Other times, he came out with a gun pointed to his head and exclaimed, "Someone give me a cigarette or I'm going to kill myself."

Some people were afraid of him, but I thought he was funny. He cracked me up laughing. However, Harley had a ferocious streak in him, too. When he was younger, he did time in prison for assaulting an officer. He got into fight with a cop, somehow managed to take his gun, and hit him with it.

Harley had an older brother who also had quite a temper. Once he was in the parking lot of a grocery store in Oakley when he met a man whom supposedly owed him some money.

He asked the man if he had the money, and the man said, "No".

Then, "Boom!"

Harely's brother put the barrel of his gun in the man's mouth and blew off his lower jaw. But amazingly the man lived. The brother went to prison, but once he got out for a couple days. I was with him and others, and we were sitting around slamming dope. It was then that he told us about the shooting.

In his own sick way, he said, "So if you ever see a man walking around without a jaw…"

But we were as sick as he was, so we laughed with him.

Harley's brother also told us that he wasn't going to stay in prison anymore. He said that he wanted to do himself in. Later, I heard that he died of a heart attack in prison.

In the few years that I was slamming dope, I had tracks going up and down my arms; it looked as if someone took a razor blade and cut into me, leaving deep scars. It wasn't always easy to shoot up when I first started. I would sit for hours poking my arms with the needle trying to find a vein. Sometimes, my arm was covered with blood. One time, I was so aggravated that I couldn't hit the right place that I thought that my veins were laughing at me and purposely moving to prevent me from getting high.

I yelled at my veins, "So you want to laugh? Laugh at this!" And I began stabbing myself repeatedly in the arm with syringe. I was trying to teach my veins a lesson! I was a bloody mess, and it took a little while to realize that I was attacking myself. With practice, I began to get better at finding veins. In fact, I became very good at it.

Aside from Harley's mean side, he was a good guy, and if he liked you, he would do whatever he could to help you. One of the reasons we were such good friends was because we both loved shooting up. But he was a little older, and he had trouble finding blood vessels. And that is where I came in. I had become an expert at it. I could find a vein with my eyes closed. In fact, they used to call me "the Doctor". Different people would come to me to help them shoot up. They would tell me that as long as I could find a blood vessel in their body, I had a free high coming.

Harley had some strange rules, and I was helping him fix some dope (shoot up). If anyone just happened to be in there at the time, he or she was not allowed to move or talk. Harley would even lock the door so no one could get up to leave. If someone had prevented me from helping him get his fix, he would have shot with his gun first and asked questions later.

Harley would put his gun next to him and tell me, "If you miss my vein, I'll kill you!"

Sometimes, he would get impatient and start moving around, making it hard to find one in his arm. I told him to hold still.

In fact, I told him, "Turn your head, and let me shoot you up in your neck."

He looked at me as if I was crazy, as he picked up his gun. I just laughed, and found the blood vessel in his arm. Once it was all done, everyone was happy and spinning. But that's how it was as long as I brought the drugs or helped him get high. I was gold!

In addition to my "medical abilities", I "knew the guy that knew the guy". I could get stuff when other people couldn't. I always knew somebody somewhere. That was my thing. People always told me that if I had put in as much time and effort into anything else besides drugs that I would be a very successful person.

O.D.

One time when I was twenty-four, I was getting high with a couple of bikers at Harley's. I was feeling pretty good, and just as a joke, I filled up a spoonful of crank and cocaine. As I mixed it up, we all laughed because it was such an enormous amount. We knew that it could be deadly, but on the other hand, if one could survive, he or she could get a real high. Everyone was standing around, but no one wanted to try it. I was so high on crank and cocaine already that I grabbed it, drew it up in a syringe, and injected it in my arm.

I thought to myself, "What did I just do?"

I can't remember what happened after that, but people told me that my eyes rolled back and I fell down. Then, I started foaming at the mouth. I could see myself falling into what appeared to be a dark hole in the ground. Then I heard children's voices. I heard hundreds of children calling me by name. I thought that maybe they were little angels calling me back from whatever darkness I was falling into. I would suddenly try to grab onto something to catch myself, but I couldn't find anything to save me. In reality, I was lying face down on the living room floor.

While on the floor, I saw myself get up out of my body. It was like watching someone else, but it was me. Actually, there was three of me. Me, watching myself on the floor; me, getting up from my body to go look out the window for the children; and I. But the window was blank. And then, the window turned dark. I was dying from an overdose and should have died, but I didn't...for a purpose.

The bikers left me there for dead. Ironically, I heard that later they both died... from drugs!

Kelly

"Kelly" was someone who I met at Harley's. Kelly was a delicate, petite and soft-spoken woman who liked to hang out around crazy bikers and drug addicts like myself.

I once told Kelly, "You should be careful who you hang around. Some of these people are a little crazy!"

She laughed and said, "That's what everybody says about you!"

Sometimes we would drive around for hours and figure out how to get high. We would drive to the river or some off road place and take turns shooting up while the other one watched for the cops.

Sometimes, Kelly would rent a motel room, and she would tell me, "Come on, let's party!"

We would get high and listen to each other talk all night long. She said that she felt safe around me because I didn't try to hit on her. She probably knew why, but she didn't say anything. Neither did I.

The last time that I saw Kelly was when she pulled up on the side of the road all excited.

"Let's party!" she exclaimed.

I said, "I can't right now; I'm waiting for someone, but I will meet you there."

It was always the same beat up motel room, but I never made it there that day. Less than a week later, I heard that Kelly was dead. It seems that the day that she tried to pick me up, she went to the motel room to shoot up, but she had some bad dope. It was cut with some kind of acid. She started feeling sick and she drove to her house where she lived with her boyfriend. She sat down next to him and began bleeding from every orifice of her body. Soon after that, she died at home. If I had met her that day, there is no doubt that I would have met the same fate.

One day, I was riding with Harley in his car through town, and we drove past a carnival.

He asked, "Do you want to stop?"

"What for?" I replied.

He pulled into the driveway, and I looked around. I saw families and people running, smiling, and having fun.

I thought to myself, "Why are all these people happy?"

"Come on!" Harley insisted.

We walked around, and Harley declared, "Let's get on a ride."

"Are you serious?" I questioned.

I didn't know how to act. Maybe I didn't know how to have fun. We got on a ride called the "Zipper". And for the next few minutes, life was exciting! I couldn't stop yelling. I glanced over at Harley as the ride zipped through the air throwing us upside-down and around. The smile on his face made me realize for a second that we were in a different world. For that short time on the ride, life was fun and exciting. In all the commotion, I didn't have time to remember all the gloom and doom.

Roswell

My parents had purchased the home in Oakley from my grandmother. All and all, my family had been in this house for fifteen years when it was just a dirt road and a field leading to Marsh Creek.

One night while my mom and aunt were enjoying a nice, quiet evening at home with my sister and her husband, suddenly a car drove by and started shooting! It came from nowhere!

"Bam!" "Bam!" "Bam!" "Bam!"

The whole front of the house was shattered. Windows were busted out and bullets were flying. One bullet flew so close by my mother that it left a burn on her arm. The bullet continued and imbedded inches away from the door to my dad's room all the way in the back. It really shook my father up, so my family packed up all their stuff and moved away without telling me. As for my father, he literally moved away and never looked back.

The night of the drive by, I was living on the streets, and a cousin just happened to be walking by.

She asked me, "Did you hear what happened?"

"No", I replied.

"Your mom's house just got shot up!" she cried.

Before she even finished the sentence, I started running towards the house. When I got there, I noticed that all the windows were shot out. I ran up to my mother and embraced her.

Dad thought I had something to do with the shooting out of anger or vengeance.

When my father heard my voice, he burst out of the house and started yelling, "Get out and don't ever come back!"

I left feeling overwhelmed and confused...and more or less abandoned. It just happened to be my birthday, and I was all alone. But soon, I ran into my best friend and explained to her what had taken place.

My friend listened compassionately and soon exclaimed, "Come to my house, and I'll throw you a party!"

I agreed, and later that night, people that I didn't even know began to arrive at her place. The next thing I knew was that she handed me a needle and a bag...Happy Birthday! I went upstairs into an empty room and shot up. I used the whole bag all at once just hoping that I would overdose and die. But "as things turned out", I passed out. When I woke up a few hours later, I realized that the needle was still in my arm and that the syringe still had drugs in it. If I had been able to push all the stuff, no doubt, I would have died.

I thought to myself, "I am still alive!"

I didn't even take the needle out. I just finished off the syringe, got up, and went on with my life.

After the drive by shooting, my parents got fed up and sold the house to my uncle.

I had met up with another cousin, and I showed her a blouse that I had found for my mother. It was a red silk blouse with a rose pattern on it. I was all excited about giving it to her.

She asked, "How are you going to get it to her?"

"What do you mean?" I questioned.

"They moved to New Mexico."

As soon as she said that, I fell to the ground and started choking. When I finally caught my breath, I began to cry. My cousin put her arms around me and began to cry, too.

"I'm sorry. I thought you knew," she sobbed.

Regardless of all the awful things my dad did to me growing up, I still needed him to love me, hold me, and teach me the things I needed to know. But he didn't.

All his actions said, "I don't care about you. You're not important enough to matter."

And I believed it.

New Mexico to me might as well have been Jupiter or Pluto. I had no idea where it was. When she said that they moved away, I felt like she said they passed away. I would never have the same relationships or the contacts from there that I had here. That day, something inside of me died. All of my dreams, all of my hopes of belonging in a family, and everything that I was searching for was gone. Even growing up, all I ever wanted to do was to make my family proud of me. That day, they all became lost hopes and dead dreams. Somehow, I was able to put those hopes and dreams on the ground and walk away. The needle became my mom and dad. It became my god. It was my reason to exist. Drugs were my life source and to take them away was like pulling the plug.

Although I may have been a victim of the needle, it was also my slave. I used it to terrorize and to destroy lives. No doubt, I was demon possessed. There were many sides to me.

There were times when I would completely black out, and when I came to, I sat there for a few hours because I couldn't remember who I was. I was clueless. At times, I would be somewhere and in the middle of a conversation, and I would think that I was somewhere else and with different people. It was confusing to them, because they didn't know what I was talking about or to whom I was talking. Other times, I would be looking around and wondering where I was and how I got there. I would wander around for a few hours or until I could remember where I was.

I was reminded of a time when I was in a friend's back yard. It was late at night, and he came out to look for me. He said that I was lying on my back dripping with sweat and with a machete in my hand.

He asked, "What are you doing?"

I responded, "They're trying to get me!"

"Who?" He questioned.

He looked around and only saw some horses next door, but in my mind, I was convinced that people were after me.

Another time, I was walking down a street and ran into a friend.

I told him, "Help me catch these guys. They're right around the corner. I can hear them, but I can't catch them!"

Later, he told me that we walked around the same block three or four times, but there was no one there. He stopped and watched me as I continued walking and talking to myself, going round and around.

I used to visit a house in another town, sometimes for days. It was all drug related. Looking back, it was all like a blur. We shot up and shot up. At one point, I was sitting in a room with a drug friend, and all of a sudden the doorbell went off. We looked at each other and laughed, because neither one of us could go to the door. I was so high that I couldn't see straight, and he was so high that he couldn't walk! They had this surveillance camera that you could see the front of the house. I started watching it and was hypnotized by it. I kept expecting to see policemen rush the front of the house, but after a few hours of staring into the tv, what were first houses, cars, and tires, slowly turned into a graveyard with demons walking around and digging their way out of the graves. I kept looking out of the blinds, thinking that the house was surrounded by demons.

I guess that my friend got tired of seeing me throw my life away, because sometimes he would look at me and suddenly start telling me, "You know, I'm not going to be alive forever to take care of you."

But to me, it was just words. Other than my needle, the world didn't exist to me. One morning, he looked out his back window and saw me throwing up.

"What's wrong," he asked.

"I need to get high," I gasped.

That must have been the final straw for him, because a few days later, he told me a story about my dad. He said that he was real sick and that he only had a week to live. At the time, my father's illness and the possibility that this may be the last time that I would be able to see him didn't really mean anything to me. But he wanted me to go see my father one last time, so he bought me a ticket so that I could fly out to see him. I really didn't want to go, but he told me that it was only for a week and that he would send me a ticket to come back.

I arrived at the Albuquerque Airport about midnight. My father and his brother had been waiting for me. Once we found each other, we went back to the truck, and I crawled in the back and fell asleep. Five hours later, they woke me up to tell me that we were there.

I opened my eyes and saw a large expanse of darkened desert with no buildings, no freeways, nothing but muted shades of gray sage, the silhouette of a mountain range on the horizon, a full moon, and blankets of stars against the charcoal blue sky. There were many more stars than at home, and they looked a lot closer. But none of the beauty of the vast desert landscape impressed me. All I wanted to see was drugs, and all I wanted to do was to get high.

We finally came to a strip that went straight through the brightly lit buildings in the town. It was like entering the Las Vegas only on a much smaller scale. We drove through the city, noticing all the UFO and alien icons and advertisements in the windows. I felt a weird, eerie sense of something going on, but I couldn't put my finger on it. We finally pulled up to my parents' trailer. It was a modest trailer that had giant, yellow sunflowers that stood like guardians in front and stretched up over the roof.

When I walked in, my mother approached and hugged me. I told her that I was just visiting. She held on to me so tight, not wanting to let go. I stood stiff as a board, not willing to show any compassion. Those feelings of love and compassion were dead.

"I'm leaving in a couple of days," I announced as I put my bags down and sat on the couch.

Then, I lay down and slept off and on for four days. When I finally woke up, I went sight seeking with my family and met relatives. It never dawned on me that Dad wasn't really sick until I tried to call my friend to get that ticket to come home. But I couldn't get through to him. In fact, he had changed his phone number. After a few days, I was able to get a hold of another friend who gave me his new number.

When I called him, he coldly asked, "What do you want?"

I told him that I wanted to come home.

"You are home!" he replied. "I didn't know what else to do, so I tricked you into going to stay with your family."

He also confessed, "I didn't want to be a part of you killing yourself anymore. The last thing I want to have to do is to pick up the phone and tell your Mom that her other son is dead, too!"

"What about all of my stuff?" I asked.

"What stuff?" he replied. "Everything is gone! The same day that you got on the plane, I cleaned out your shed and threw everything that you owned away. It was like you never existed."

I tried to plead with him to let me come back, but he didn't want to hear anything I had to say.

All I remember is that he said, "Take care of yourself."

Then, he hung up. That's when it hit me. I was stuck in this strange place, home seemed like a million miles away, and I couldn't even begin to think which way to start walking. My crushed hope of returning home was the worst. I felt like smashing my face in the cement, and I wanted to rip off my skin. I screamed and punched myself, pulling out my hair. I threw myself on the ground like a fish out of water. Then suddenly, I stopped because I found it was getting hard to breathe. I wonder what the neighbors thought seeing me thrash around in the dirt?

My weird feelings about this town continued. Once my mother told us about a dream she had about aliens that were crawling around in the living room. One of the aliens had my sister on his shoulders and was taking her out the window. My brother in law was amazed, because he had the same dream. He just didn't want to mention it because he thought that everyone would think he was crazy.

The days were long and hot, and I was depressed because I was so far away from home. I would often sit outside and stare at the weird desert creatures. My thoughts were filled with death and all the different ways to die. I had been in Roswell a few weeks, and my hopes of getting back to California were getting farther and farther away. One day as I was sitting outside, a car pulled up. It was a young guy with a big smile.

"I'm your cousin," he yelled.

He said that someone had called him and said that he had a cousin from California, so he wanted to show me around town. Before he finished talking, I was already getting in his car.

"Let's go!" I cried.

We drove off, and he asked, "What do you like to do?"

"I'm an addict," I replied. "I like to shoot dope. I need a hit!"

"All I have is some weed and some beer," he answered.

"Well, I guess that's something," I said.

So we drove off to his house, smoked weed, and drank. His girlfriend, her brother, and the next door neighbor were there. I was related to a lot of people in town, however, there was a lot of animosity within the family. Everyone was divided up on different sides, and because of my last name, if I walked up to the wrong group, I could have been seriously beaten or even shot. I guess it didn't help that I was from California and that I was all punked out. It wasn't every day that people saw someone with a Mohawk walking down their streets. But I didn't care. I wasn't into their alliances or family wars. I was just trying to figure out how to get high.

Among the people I had come to know, incest was not uncommon, and relatives slept with each other. Murders and other crimes seemed all too familiar. Alliances and wars within the family were prevalent. During the first month I was there, I went to eleven funerals.

As the hot, dry, and sandy days dragged on, I began meeting new people, and drinking became my new high. Every day was a party. The strange thing was that in this town, businesses stopped selling alcohol at noon on Saturday and all day Sunday. So we had to make sure that we had enough before the liquor stores closed.

My friend's mother was a serious alcoholic, so she usually had gallons of hard liquor hidden away. But my friend and I would come in and start searching the house until we found every drop of it. After a while, she got tired of playing cat and mouse games with the liquor, so she started drinking with us. On a typical day, we would all sit around and drink a gallon of vodka and a case of beer before noon. I don't know what they were all running from that they would try to get so far away from reality, but I could remember so clearly that the life I lived seemed very far away.

I remember one morning getting so drunk that I passed out in the middle of the street and fell face down in the snow. My friends picked me up, dragged me into the house, and I slept it off, only to get up and start all over again.

Another time, I was walking along with a friend, and I told him, "Watch!"

Then, I ran through the intersection and right up to a car that was stopped at the red light. And "BAM!" I kicked the car as hard as I could, jumped up and down, screamed and laughed. I remember the look of complete fear in that poor lady's face.

"Imagine some drunk, demon-possessed, crazy man with a big Mohawk coming out of nowhere and kicking your car and acting wild!"

She drove off, and I waved goodbye.

Once, I managed to start a fight with the whole neighborhood. I was severely outnumbered, but drunk and upset. So, I called for someone to come get me. When they did, I was still out there in people's faces and arguing.

When I saw my ride, I ran to the car and started yelling, "Kill them! Run over them! Run over them!"

I screamed that over and over, but my ride just laughed.

Once we were getting drunk, and the girl next door came up to us with a young man and said, "Hey Eli, this is your cousin 'Tim.'"

We met and I asked him if he wanted a drink. He agreed. A few hours went by, and we were all drunk; then, one by one, we passed out. Later that night, I woke up and noticed that Tim was trying to make a move on my friend whom I will call "Johnny". Johnny became very uncomfortable, so he got up and left the room. That is when Tim and I slept together. I really didn't care that he was my cousin. I knew exactly what I was doing, and I knew that it was wrong. But

I didn't care. I didn't even try to blame it on the alcohol. I didn't care if it made God mad. I had gotten to a point in my life where nothing mattered.

I also imagined what it would be like to be raped, tortured, and killed by Jeffery Dalmer, the serial killer. That shows how low I had sunk and how much I had fallen into a dark, dark world.

A few months later, I learned that my aunt, my mother, and my sister were going back to California for a visit. I got all excited about the prospects of going with them, so I started packing my bags.

"Finally, I am going back home!" I thought.

Home to me wasn't a house; it was everything I knew.

When my family saw that I was getting my things together, they questioned, "What are you doing?"

"I'm getting ready!" I said.

"Oh, no!" they responded. "You're not going. You have to stay here with your father."

I argued for a while, but it didn't matter. They went on to California without me.

The day they left, my dad and I went for a ride. Of course, he was drunk, so I had to drive. We drove around, then, we stopped and he introduced me to more cousins and family members. We were in the front of a house talking to a bunch of people, and I looked over at him. He was so drunk that he was holding a beer with one hand and onto a tree with the other hand so that he wouldn't fall over. All of a sudden, he started to urinate in his pants like nothing was happening. He didn't even stop talking. I looked around at everybody, but one of the ladies told me that it was all right.

I laughed and declared, "Well, if he doesn't care, I don't care."

But I really was embarrassed, not only for him, but also for myself. Looking back, I think that my father was just as messed up in his mind as I was.

I guess in a normal situation, I would have been happy living with my family. I had a home. I had food. I could have had a regular life, but that was not what I was looking for. I just wanted to get high again. So once I got the chance to leave Roswell, I took it. I had spent nine months there, and I was more than eager to leave. My sister traveled back and forth all the time, so I asked if I could catch a ride with her, and she agreed. Getting in the car, I realized that I would be coming back to absolutely nothing. I wouldn't have any money, no food, nor a place to live. But that didn't matter. It was worth it to me. All I could think about was sticking a needle in my arm. I had gotten nauseous from meth before. But it was unusual for me to feel sick to my stomach. However, during the ride, I got so excited just thinking about the rush that I almost started throwing up. I had to force myself to sleep to keep from getting sick.

I woke up to my sister's voice saying that we were here. I told her to just drop me off wherever. She pulled over, I got out, and we went our separate ways. I made my way over to Harley's in Knightsen.

Harley was surprised to see me, but the first thing that he did was to say "welcome home", and he handed me a full syringe.

"Yup. I was home!"

Four or five years after my mother and aunt went to visit in California, my mother left my father. She had put up with so much. She had done all that she could to hold the marriage together and she was a very good mother to us kids, but she couldn't put up with my father's drinking and his poor behavior anymore, and she moved back to California with my aunt.

Reconnecting

It wasn't long before I ran into my friend whom had originally sent me to Roswell. At first, I was mad and really didn't want to talk to him. He lied to me, sent me away for the last nine months in the desert, and got rid of all my stuff. I was hurt, but even in all of that, there wasn't anything that getting high couldn't fix. Moreover, I wasn't trying to carry anything like anger or hurt; it was enough just to carry myself through the day. After getting a fix, everything went back to normal, and I ended up leaving town with my friend. He always had somewhere for me to stay until he didn't need me anymore. Then, I wouldn't see him until he needed me again.

My friend had a house out of town where he lived with his girlfriend, who was a nurse with a good education and a good job. He had a large backyard, which was just a field. But he used some other guys and I to build sidewalks, a driveway, and to do landscaping. He divided the yard by putting up a fence so that when you looked out his back window, you would see a nice normal backyard. But beyond the fence was the rest of the yard, which was desolate and dry with rusty wire fencing and a couple beat-up abandoned cars and an egg-shaped trailer. That is where I lived, basically like a "throw away".

One day, he took me into town, and he hung out with his buddies at a house where everyone was drinking. I wasn't allowed to talk to his friends, hang out with them, or take a ride with them unless he was there. The reason for this was because these guys were the type to make life changing decisions without thinking. In other words, they were hardcore criminals.

I was with my friend, so it was o.k. for me to have a good time by having a couple of drinks, laughing, and dancing. But the next thing I knew, I was waking up in the little trailer in the backyard. I must have passed out, because when I woke up, I noticed that I had a needle in one hand and bag in the other.

The trailer was old and beat up with no water or electricity. Once in a while, I was able to hook up a water hose so that I could wash my clothes in a bucket or take a bath. I shared the backyard with three pit bulls. The funny thing was that the dogs ate better than I did. I knew, because I fed them. Sometimes, if my friend didn't come in the yard, I would just sit there day after day without food or water. He locked all the gates from the outside so that I couldn't get out. Besides, if I did, where would I have gone? He lived in the middle of nowhere. But I think that what he was trying to do was to teach me a lesson. He was trying to break me.

He tried to make life as an addict unbearable as he could so that I would say, "I give up! It's not worth it to live like this."

But I wasn't willing to be broken. It was worth it to me to be punished, tortured, used as a puppet, and disrespected. It was worth it to me to be dirty and hungry, to have no meaning just to get a hit or a fix every once in a while. All that mattered was putting a needle in my arm.

I wasn't allowed to walk to the house unless I was called, so I wandered in the backyard in search for water to mix with drugs. Usually if I didn't have a spoon, I would use the bottom of a tin can to stir it up. And if I didn't have a can, I would put water in the bag with a piece of cotton or a cigarette filter. Sometimes, I would use a piece of a sock or anything I could use for a filter. Then, I would draw the mix up in the needle. But not this time. I couldn't find water. However, I did find a bag of trash, and I found an old bottle of orange juice. I didn't know how long it had been there, nor did I care. I mixed it with the drugs and shot up. A couple of hours later, I dug through the garbage bag again and found a bottle of liquor and used that to slam the drugs.

A couple of weeks later, my friend moved a bigger trailer in his yard and told me that a friend of his was moving in. So at least now, I would have someone to talk to. That friend was a woman I will call "Tina". Once Tina moved in, things changed. There were people around… like a party, and everybody was doing their own thing. But it wasn't always like that. Once, it was just she and I. We were very hungry, and we really wanted to go into town to get something to eat. She asked if anybody was in the house. I said that didn't know, and we agreed to try knocking at the door. Tina then went to the front and knocked. Nobody answered. We decided to borrow the man's vehicle that he had parked in the yard to go to find food. I was excited that I was going to be able to leave my "prison yard", so we drove to one of her friend's house in town. There we ate a sandwich and were all happy. Then we started hitting the glass pipe.

All of a sudden, the phone rang. Tina and I looked at each other.

Tina's friend told us that there was no way that the man could know where we were.

She thought we were dumb when we said, "Don't answer the phone!"

But Tina's friend answered the phone. And it was him! It was strange, but it seemed like this guy had eyes and ears everywhere!

He exclaimed, "Let me talk to Tina!"

He knew we were there. We knew we were in trouble, because one, I was told not to leave the yard, and two, she knew not to take me anywhere. Third, we weren't supposed to use his vehicle. All we wanted was to eat, but the man didn't see it that way. In complete anger, he told Tina that he lit her car on fire. Her car had been broken down in his front yard. He was so mad that he told her not to come back to the house with me because he was going to kill me. He wasn't used to me being disobedient. Out of complete fear, I told

Tina to drop me off a block away from his house so that I could go back to Oakley, thirty miles away.

She asked me how I was going to get there.

I said, "I don't know, but I'm not going back the house!"

And so I started walking back to Oakley to get away from him. I remember looking back and thinking that the man was going to come looking for me. I didn't think he was going to kill me, but I wasn't sure what he would do. He grew up in a town where it was "dog eat dog", "kill or be killed". He was known all over and was well respected, or should I say feared? It took me all day and all night to get to Oakley, but even though it was long and hot, I walked as fast as I could. I remember thinking that I wasn't going to make it. At one point, I had to go to the bathroom. I tried to hold it, but it wasn't long before I had to run into the middle of the field to relieve myself. Struggling to understand why I was in this situation, I began to cry in desperation. I walked back to the road and threw myself down to rest. Just then, I looked up and before me was a snake that was slithering right towards me! Life just wasn't getting any better. I jumped up and started running!

After traveling all that time, I arrived back at Harley's. But before I could get to the front door to knock, a car drove up next to me. And you guessed it! It was my friend!

I didn't know what to expect. He just looked at me for a minute; then he said, "Your mom is looking for you. Get in, and I will take you to her."

I don't know why he said that. I guess that was his way of apologizing. So, I got in the car, and we drove off. He was silent, and so was I. There were times when I honestly thought that he wanted to kill me and that I was in great danger around him and his friends, but then there were times that I felt extremely safe around him. I was his puppet; it didn't matter what I thought or what I had to say. I just did whatever he said to do and went wherever he told me to go. I had to hide my homosexual lifestyle when I was around him. It was easier to be a slave or a puppet than to let him know who I was because I feared that he would have me killed. As long as he fed me drugs, I was willing to stay in that prison of a yard. Before I knew it, we pulled up to his house through the backyard. He slipped into his house, and I trudged through the brush-filled yard to my little beat up trailer.

One of the things that my friends liked doing was to drive around, pick up hookers, and take turns sleeping with them. About five of us were a van, and we picked up a woman, drove around, and everyone took turns with her. Just as I feared, my friend told me that it was my turn. I started talking about being too high and not being high enough. I was trying not to make any sense. I just knew that they were going to catch on, and I feared that they might kill me because they didn't understand. He pulled over and let the woman out, and we drove off. Nobody said a word.

Not long afterwards, Harley died, leaving a wife and two sons. My friend wanted me to stay near his widow in a trailer park in another county to make sure that they had a way to survive. She was having trouble conducting a business, and she needed protection from bad deals as people were supposedly robbing her.

I lived in an abandoned, old trailer on the other side of the park from her. The trailer didn't have water or electricity, but it was a roof over my head. I washed my clothes and took a bath in a bucket of water that I brought over from the other trailers. But business was good.

There were other people selling drugs in the trailer court, and each of them had their own clientele. But I was different from the other dealers. While the others were cold and about themselves, I was more about understanding my customers and their pain. I even let people who didn't have any place to stay spend the night or nights in the trailer with me. I also fed them. I realized that people came to get high so that they didn't have to feel their pain. Word got around that I would charge any amount...whatever the people had. I did not want to turn anyone away empty handed, even trading for broken down items.

My sales quickly doubled, and before I knew it, other people went out of business in the trailer court because everyone was coming to me. All the money I made went straight to Harley's widow. I wasn't allowed to keep any, but I noticed that she was spending a lot of money on other things, leaving us dry. So I quickly went to other connections and continued on.

Harley's widow saw that I was making other deals. She wanted me either to leave the trailer or buy it off of her. So I bought it from her. It was more or less scrap metal, but I didn't have anywhere else to go. After a few weeks went by, another connection came by and saw that business was still going, and he had a discussion with the widow and I about the money she still owed him. She told him in secret that he could have the trailer. I never thought about a pink slip. She gave it to him! Remember, this was a beat up, junk trailer, which didn't have any use to anyone except me because it was my home, but I found myself in a position where I had two choices: pay the connection for the trailer or get out.

I explained to him that I had already bought it, but he said that he owned it because he had the pink slip. I couldn't argue with him about that, so I paid him for it. This was the second time I bought it.

The next morning, a man knocked on the front of the trailer. As I went out, he began to tell me that the "owner" called and wanted the trailer scrapped. After arguing with him, all I could do was to watch as he hooked up my only home and towed it off with whatever I owned in it. One of the lessons learned was to never try to deal for other people when you belong to someone already. Don't eat, breathe, or speak unless you are told to. The more disobedient you are, the bigger the punishment. But I was stubbornly strong. People could do anything to me that they could: humiliate me and disrespect me, but the one thing that they could not do was to break me.

After the trailer incident, I was homeless again.

Chapter 4

The Garage

ꕥ

The garage was known as "The Party House". All kinds of gang activities, parties, and fights went on in there, and it was open to anyone and everyone. There was no door on the garage, so anyone could just walk in.

The garage was like a circus. You never know what was going to happen. There were often forty to fifty people there at one time, and the whole street would be full of cars. There would be rival gang members. People were getting high, partying, and fighting. Drive-bys occurred. People shot at the garage. Sometimes, people called it the "Mental House", because they thought everyone in there was insane.

At times, people were overdosing. One girl was hauled off in an ambulance because she had been running up and down the street screaming that she had been raped. The next day, a guy was taken to the hospital for a drug overdose. Later, a girl was stabbed. One guy had gotten cut with a machete, and another one was trying to dig out a bullet from his arm. The strange thing was that the crazier it got, the more people were attracted to the garage and didn't want to leave. It was like a system of chaos, which lasted a little more than three years. People hung out in the yard all night long. Some stayed in abandoned cars and some even pitched tents on the lawn.

Besides, all the drug traffic, it was also a hangout for a well-known gang. It was funny, because my connections were members of a rival gang. The money was good, so everybody understood that the garage was neutral ground. But one wrong move, and it would have definitely been a blood bath. One cop told a guy that whoever is selling drugs there must have a lot of power because with anyone else, there would have been blood. But it wasn't about me or anyone else having power; it was the about the power of addiction that suppressed any hate or animosity that people may have had for each other. With my own eyes, I saw addiction overpower hate and rivalry.

One would have hoped that it was because of a more noble cause, but drugs broke the barrier between rival gangs. Drugs made people happy in this false world, and they would come and go just to get high. Rival gangs shared the same pipe. There were a number of times that I sat between rival gang members. I would sit with "Red Raggers, Blue Raggers", "White Supremacist", and others. For me, it wasn't about being in a gang or having a big name. It wasn't even about the money. For me, it was about the drugs, because with them, I could numb myself and escape from reality. I wasn't interested in being in one gang or another. I had friends on both sides. Whereas some people only dealt with their own kind, I didn't want to limit myself.

"Why have a piece of the cake when you can have it all?" I thought.

Along with the rest of them, I was there for the high.

The owner of the house and the garage had four kids; two of them were girls in their late teens, and the boys were older. But he was usually away at his girlfriend's house. So there was basically no adult supervision.

Sometimes, we would be in the house. One friend used to hang out with us. One day, his mother, a little old Spanish woman, came to the house and banged on the door. We thought it was the police. Somehow, she made her way inside and stormed around the house, looking for her son. She burst through the doors of all the rooms, found him, and dragged him out by the hair while she screamed something in Spanish. The next thing we knew, he was in Mexico. We were the crowd that your mother always warned you about!

Most of the time when I was in the garage, it was full of junk: front to back, top to bottom. I would move garbage on top of garbage to make a place to sit or sleep. I arranged a couch and chairs to make it look kind of like an apartment... well, an apartment surrounded by junk. There were no other doors, no windows, and no electricity, but I made the best of it. During the first few days that I was by myself in the garage, I was never really alone. There were rats, snakes, maggots, lizards, and an occasional opossum...and of course, demons. At night, I would smoke crystal meth and fight those creatures that would crawl all over me until the sun came up. I remember that one time when I woke up, I felt something chewing on my neck. It was a rat!

I had learned that the best way to keep supplied in drugs was to sell them. If I didn't get the cash, I would take something in on trade. I got some beautiful items: china, lamps, furniture, etc. But I wasn't interested in any of these things. All I cared about was what they could get me. Drugs. The more, the better. 150% of my energy went towards getting high.

I had everything I wanted: money, drugs, and more things than I knew what to do with. When you walked in the backyard, it would look like a mini city dump with abandoned cars and trash that consisted of everything you could think of. Then, when you entered the garage...on a good day, you would see state of the art electronic equipment, maybe a Persian rug, antique wall shelves full of crystal vases and figurines, hanging lamps, and matching furniture. I remember sitting on the floor one day with drugs all around me.

I thought, "This is as good as it gets."

I couldn't imagine life any other way. I got so high that I thought I could laugh at God.

"Who needs God?" I would ask.

I was doing this all by myself. So I thought. But things were subject to change, not just by the day, hour, or minute, but by the second. One moment was all it took, and I would blow up in a rage, swinging, throwing, and destroying anything I could get my hands on. Everything would be completely demolished, and I would throw it into a pile in the middle of the garage. Next, I'd lie on the pile of broken wood and glass. I would just lay there for hours and drift off somewhere in my mind. Then, I would gather all the broken pieces and throw them in the backyard to accumulate. It was a real mess! But by the next day, I would have the garage completely re-furnished with all brand new stuff. Nothing really lasted in the garage for more than two or three days. Things either got stolen, or I destroyed them. Sometimes, I would destroy them just so they would not be stolen.

People would usually root through the remnants in the backyard or in the garage, because a lot of stuff that I would throw out there would still be good. Moreover, I often just didn't have any room for these things.

During a high, I could deny my need of God, but I had an out of control emptiness that also couldn't deny. As things built up, I felt the need to get away. Everything was going so fast, and I could feel my mind breaking apart. A friend of mine told me about this place he owned in the country. He gave me the address, and another friend and I drove there. We pulled up to this huge house that was condemned. It was boarded up, and weeds were growing everywhere out of control. But it was the address he gave me. As we walked in, we saw that the house was full of furniture, but there was no electricity. I had a strange eerie feeling about the place. It was almost like a paralyzing fear that came over me. But I was glad to be away from the garage.

As night came, we had to use flashlights to see. I noticed that a man lived in the house. I went up to him and explained who I was and that my friend owned the property. He just looked at me, but he never responded. In fact, in the three days that we were there, he never spoke at all. I remember sitting in the dark room hearing people talking and walking through the residence. I walked around the house with a flashlight. Nobody was there. Every once in a while, somebody would walk past me. I was too afraid to talk. It could have been that I just sat there all night paralyzed with fear. After the third day, I couldn't take it anymore, I left the house and everything I had taken with me. I just left things there. It wasn't worth it to go back in the house. Nothing about those three days made any sense, nor could I explain them. I made my way back to the garage. At least, in the garage, I could recognize my demons.

From a Nice Lady to an Addict

Once, we were in the garage with the normal crowd of drug addicts and thugs. We were just kind of hanging out. I was shooting up, and the rest of the guys were taking turns smoking the glass pipe. In walked a friend with a very attractive, well-dressed lady who could have been a model. Not a strand of her hair was out out of place.

I asked, "What's your name?"

She said, "Sue."

"Sue, what are you doing here?" I questioned. "You're a little bit out of place, don't you think? Are you here to get high, because you don't look the part?"

"I'm here with my boyfriend, and this will be my first time," she replied all excited.

She had no idea.

"I'm just asking because you don't fit the description of the every day street trash that I see come through here," I cautioned. I was never too tactful when choosing my words, nor did I care.

But after looking at and talking to her, I realized that addiction doesn't depend on descriptions. She was "Movie Star Sue", because of her striking appearance. But that didn't matter. Drugs are great equalizers. They can and do consume all walks of life, and they can bring anyone down.

I was then reminded of another woman who didn't fit the description of an addict. I was helping a friend in another town at the time. My friend had just purchased some duplex apartments, and he let me stay in one while we fixed them up. The apartments were located in a gang related, heavy drug active area. It was mostly African American and Hispanic. During the day it was usually all right, but at night it was like the whole picture changed and it became an entirely different place.

The first couple nights were the worst. In order to get to the apartment door, I had to walk past a group of guys selling crack cocaine. It didn't matter that there was no television in the duplex, because I could just sit in the dark all night and listen to them handle their business. I used to watch their shadows on the closed curtains in the window. They were my entertainment, but I didn't want them to know it. One night, I noticed that it was kind of quiet, and I didn't see any shadows. I thought that it was kind of strange, so I peeked out of the window to see what was going on. Across the street was a house that was all boarded up. Some of the street-lights were busted out, and there was glass all over. Seeing the people in the house reminded me of roaches going in and out. They looked robotic, like zombies. It was 3:00 a.m.

What was crazy about it was that there were different types of people frequenting the house. The crack dealers had this community programmed and under control. But it only took a few days for people living in the apartment to start coming through to get meth from me instead of crack from those in the house.

What was really shocking was that one of the clients who came the house across the street was a very petite white woman wearing a suit and carrying a purse and a brief case. She walked into the crack house as nonchalantly as if she was entering a grocery store. She made whatever business deal she wanted to make, then she walked out and back down the dark street as if she didn't have a care in the world. That really surprised me. I thought that the whole area was ghetto and dangerous,. I didn't feel safe even behind locked doors, and here she was out in the open! But she seemed oblivious to the danger around her.

The day before, I was getting high in the apartment.

When I walked outside, one of the neighbors approached me and said, "Hey, did you see what just happened?"

"No, what?" I asked.

"There was a man with a machine gun standing right in front of your door," he explained. "The cops came and were finally able to wrestle him down and take him to jail. The whole thing lasted about an hour."

I told him that I had no idea. I was busy shooting up inside.

And that was in the daytime. It only got worse, the later it got.

I looked at the house all night, and asked myself if the people were completely unaware of the danger they were putting themselves in. But who was I to talk? I am sure that if I were someone else looking at me live my life, I would be shocked at what I was putting myself through.

As the months went by, and Sue used repeatedly, I noticed that the drugs started to affect her, not only in her appearance but also in the way she acted. She was becoming like the rest of us. It didn't take long for her boyfriend to run off with someone else, leaving her in this big, dark drug world.

One night, it was kind of late, and I was walking through an alley. From around the corner, I heard a commotion. It was Sue! She was a mess! She had been up for days, and it showed. Her hair was all crazy, and it looked like she hadn't changed her clothes in a long time. She didn't have any make-up on, and she didn't even have any shoes.

"Have you seen my boyfriend?" she cried in desperation.

I told her that I hadn't seen him.

"Oh, he's around here somewhere," she yelled. "I can hear him talking. I can hear his voice. He's in one of these apartments!"

Then, she began to scream for him to come outside. I stood back and watched her run back and forth from apartment to apartment yelling his name.

I had seen the destruction and decay in Sue's life in just a few short months. Drugs had taken control of her life and had brought her down. She used to be vibrant, in control, and in charge of herself. But now she was just an empty shell, driven by the control of her addiction.

I approached her and said, "Sue, stop and look at yourself. Look at what you have become. You don't deserve this kind of life. You could have or do anything in life. All you have to do is to walk away. Don't become like me."

Then I turned and left.

I always wondered what became of Sue. Was she dead like so many drug addicts? Or did she wind up in jail? Was she on the streets?

A few years went by, and as I was walking down the street one day, I stopped by a red light. As I was waiting for the light to change, a beautiful, new car drove up next to me. As I looked up, my eyes connected with Sue's. She looked like she used to, full of life and with a sparkle back in her eyes. She was with a new man in a nice car, and I knew she was living a new life. Just then, the light turned green, and the car began to drive off. Without moving or letting the man sitting next to her have any idea that she knew me, she winked to let me know that she was o.k.

I couldn't help but smile. In my heart, I knew that she had made it out. I wished that for myself, but I knew that my addiction was too strong. After a few minutes, I just put my head down and continued to walk.

More Incidents in the Garage

Once I got an infection in my arm from shooting up dope. Usually, I could slice the infection or drain it with a needle, but not this time. I stabbed it and cut it with razor blades, but it was too badly infected. After a few days went by, a guy told me that if I didn't go to a doctor, he was going to call 911. More days passed, and I started to get a little worried because it wasn't getting any better. I finally went to the doctor. At first, I saw the nurse, and she asked me what happened. I said that I was bitten by a spider.

She looked at me and asked, "Was it a spider or a needle?"

"Either, or," I replied.

When the doctor came in after a few minutes, he looked at my arm and was quiet. After finished examining it, he said that he was going to cut my arm and clean it out. However, he also cautioned that there was a good chance that they would have to amputate.

"Amputate? What's that?" I asked.

"There is a good possibility that your arm will have to be cut off," he replied.

"Agh!" I gasped.

It felt like I just got punched in the neck. It was my worst fear.

I asked, "How will I shoot up with one arm?"

The doctor looked at me in disbelief, closed the curtain, and walked away. But he did return and cleaned it out, leaving a hole in my arm as big as a tennis ball.

One day, I had a serious pain in my foot. I sat on the side of the road, pulled off my boot to see if I could figure out what was wrong with it. I took off my sock along with a top layer of skin. I looked at it, and it actually scared me because it didn't even look like a foot. It looked more like a mass of mutilated meat. I quickly put my sock and boot back on.

I started thinking, "Oh man, my feet are rotten and are probably going to have to be cut off. Now I am going to have to hustle harder so that I can pay somebody to push me up and down the road in a wheel chair so that I can continue my business."

That was all I cared about.

The worse situations got in my life, the more I just continued down my destructive path. It never dawned on me to walk away and change my life. I didn't know that there was an option. It was just easier to let my mind adjust to the situation, however bad it got. I figured it was just another day in the life of an addict.

Speed, meth, and crystal were my choice of drug, but I would do anything: PCP, angel dust, cocaine, crack, LSD, heroine, etc. Such a person is known as a "garbage can". Sometimes, on a bad day when I didn't have anything to slam, I would draw blood from my arm with a needle and shoot it back up. "Cotton fever" is when a person gets a piece of cotton in the needle, shoots it, and it travels through one's blood system. It makes one's bones hurt and body tighten. All one wants to do is to curl up in a ball in agony. The best way to get rid of it is to shoot up again; otherwise the person has to deal with the pain for a few hours.

I must have looked strange with all the sores and infections all over me. Trails of dried blood were all over my arms.

Once a friend of mine walked in and asked, "What are you doing?"

I had a bad habit of digging into my skin and making sores on my head and face. Then later, I would go back and pick the scabs. But this time, I got carried away. I said that I was trying to take the skin off the side of my head. My friend looked disgusted as I laughed with blood coming down my face.

I told him, "You can stab me, you can shoot me, you can even light me on fire, but if you try to take my dope, that's where I draw the line."

One time, a cousin of the neighbor came over to visit. We invited him into the garage and got him high. And that was all it took. He was addicted. He soon moved into the garage and partied with us all the time. But that was one invitation that turned terribly wrong.

Looking at this guy was like seeing Linda Blair from the "Exorcist", but without the makeup. He had this evil grin for a smile, and he had empty eyes and a blank look on his face. Sometimes, he would stare at the walls, and every so often, his expression would change and he would turn into a completely different person. In fact, if I talked to him, he wouldn't answer, but sometimes, if I stood up, he would mimic me. When I moved my arm, he moved his. When I talked, he mumbled over my voice. One time, I was so fearful that I tried to run out of the garage, but he ran in front of me and just stood there. I wasn't afraid of him; I was afraid of the demons in him. But "afraid" isn't even the word. I was "tormented" by them.

One night, he woke me up by kicking the couch. He was walking back and forth next to me with a hammer in his hand. He told me that he had heard voices instructing him to kill me and that I would not see the sun come up. I would be dead before morning. This went on for four hours. I was lying down, and he was over me chanting it over and over. He said that if I moved, he had been told to charge and beat me with the hammer.

I figured that I needed to act crazier than he was in order to show him that I wasn't afraid. And really, that wasn't too hard for me to do!

I reached for the hammer and yelled, "If you're going to kill me, then kill me!"

He was startled, and I saw my chance to escape. So I did. I started running out the front, and I got away. Phheww!

I was leery about coming back to the garage, not knowing what to expect. But that was my home, so I had to return. When I finally came back the next day, I found that he was sitting on the couch as usual. His personality had changed, and he was acting like his usual self. I knew he had been controlled by demons that night.

Years later, I saw the same man on Bart. He was in a wheel chair. I talked to him, asking what had happened. He relayed a story that was not unlike the stories of other druggies I had known. Driven by his addiction, he had tried to rob some drug dealer at an apartment in Pittsburg. He jumped out the window and off the balcony, and one of the other guys shot him in the back. He has been paralyzed ever since.

There was a house up the road and a group of guys.

I met them once, and one of them told me, "You know, why would we go out or watch t.v. when we could just pull up some chairs, drink a couple beers, and watch the action that was going on in the garage. Tv didn't have any shows on that exciting!"

Sometimes, the police would block off the streets and bring in the dogs and helicopters. They would have fifteen or twenty of us laying face down in the street just like in the movies. The cops always came well prepared, I guess because of all the gang members who were hanging out.

At times, I would hide from the officers. I would bury myself in the garbage and stay there for hours until it was safe.

Martinez

But I was not always able to hide. Once, several of us were sitting around in the garage getting high. All of a sudden the cops came in. I had an ounce in my pocket, some syringes and pipes all over, and a bag on the table. I admitted that whatever they found was mine. They searched everyone and let them go except for one guy whom they took to the side. This seemed strange to me.

"What were they talking about?" I wondered.

But I really thought I knew. I thought that he was ratting me out.

As I stood there alone and in handcuffs, the guy stepped forward and said, "The bag belongs to me."

The cops told him to leave, but he insisted. So, they finally arrested him, too. He told me that if I took all the blame, the charges would have been more severe. And he said that he didn't want me to go to jail by myself. That kind of blew me away, because everyone else was more than happy to leave me behind.

We were both taken to the county jail in Martinez for possession.

As I was being arrested, I had vivid flashbacks of my life. I saw myself as a little boy, my family, and especially my mom. I honestly felt that I would never get to see my family again. When we got there, we were booked together, but the other guy was separated right away due to his gang affiliation.

I remember asking, "Where did he go?"

But I was released to the general population. That wouldn't have been so bad, except that the other inmates thought that I was in the same gang as the other guy, which could be like a death sentence. But I wasn't, nor was I in any gang, as mentioned. So now I had another problem besides being in jail: the inmates thought I was in a rival gang.

And it only got worse.

Soon they brought in a cellmate. When I first saw him in the holding cell, he was curled up in a ball on the floor. When they put him in my cell, he seemed o.k., but then he started having convulsions. We had bunk beds; I was on the top bunk, and he was on the bottom. I could feel this man kick on the bottom of my bunk. Then, his body began to flop around like a fish. He was seizing. There was a sheet wrapped around the top of his head and body. He looked ghost-like as he thrashed around the cell, hitting his head on things. Then he was quiet. He died!

The deputies rushed in and noticed all the bruises on his body from convulsing. After separating me while the medics came in, they escorted me to the center room with the other inmates. The center room had beds, and around the room were two man cells. The stench was like rancid clothes and body odor. As they brought me in, everyone gathered around to see what was going on. It was then that they rolled my former cellmate out in a body bag. Of course, they thought that I had killed him because I was supposedly in a rival gang. And the word spread throughout the jail community.

By then, it was almost morning. A detective came to me. I was questioned and accused of murder. I was asked what I had in my hand; what was I beating him with while he was asleep? I was scared to death, because there were no witnesses, and I knew that I could be charged with killing this man. And that is exactly what they did.

After that, I had a vision. I saw the hall extend and extend like in a dream. What that said to me was that I was going to go from this place to a worse one… forever… because I couldn't see the end.

"You're not going to do this to me," I silently spoke to the officers. "You can't accuse me of something I didn't do."

My first impulse was to grab the deputy's weapon and to shoot myself. I figured that it was my only option. So, I suddenly reached for the gun. But the deputy struggled with me, and I was never able to reach it.

The gang members in the jail had already tried and convicted me of killing one of there own.. You can't really see anyone in the other cells, but I could hear them talking among themselves. They were placing bets on who would kill me when the deputies switched shifts. We were quite a few stories up, and they kept saying that someone would throw me over the rail. My bed was right next to the rail outside the cell, and whenever someone walked by, I thought they were coming to kill me. I thought that I would either go to prison and someone in that gang would kill me there or that I would die right there…"over the rail".

I told a guard that I didn't feel safe there because the other prisoners thought that I wore different colors and that they believed I killed someone in their gang.

He looked at me, kind of laughed, and said, "Go back to your bunk."

I felt like I was in a hopeless situation.

I didn't know what else to do, so I cried out to God, "If you get me out of this mess, I promise I will never get high again!"

That was my life: getting high. In my mind, I prepared myself for the worst. I felt they were going to kill me. But the next morning, something amazing happened.

An officer came to me and announced, "Roll up you bed, you're leaving!"

I was released!

No explanations. Not another word. Just that I was free to go. That was like a miracle to me. I was so relieved. I couldn't believe that I was leaving this place and it wasn't in a body bag.

But I wasn't really free. I forgot my promise to God, and I went back into the prison of my addiction.

Interestingly enough, one of the prisoners had told me something that night that was really good advice.

He said, "Maybe you should lay off drugs."

That was just another warning, this time from the mouth of a cellmate. But, of course, I didn't listen.

I remember getting picked up, and I just said, "After all I have been through, I need to get high", not even thinking twice about what I had promised to God.

Surprise Meeting with my Cousin

It didn't take long to get back into circulation. As the days went on, things only got worse. The parties got bigger, the traffic got heavier, and it was non-stop. There were times when I would hide myself under an abandoned car outside just to get away from everybody. Another time, I locked myself in the garage with a chain and locks that was covered by a piece of wood. And do you think that that stopped people? I heard a noise on the roof, and to my surprise, a couple of guys decided to take the roof apart to get in. Compute the madness.

Dealers from all over started visiting me, trying to get me to sign contracts. Others would come with guns telling me that I was in danger and that I was supposed to go with them so that they could hide me out. One time, some guys came and introduced themselves. Later, one of them told me that the night they came over, they had the garage surrounded with men who were armed and ready to shoot because of all the things they heard about the "garage". These were all people that I had never seen before, and most of them I never saw again.

What started out as just trying to escape reality turned into something that was way beyond my control or more than anything I could have imagined. And I didn't know how to stop it. After getting raided the last time with the help of those who came through the roof, I left the garage and never went back...which led me to the streets. But it seemed like everywhere I went, people followed me.

If I stopped at someone's house, a half an hour later, the parking lot was full, and I'd have to leave because the people living there didn't want that kind of trouble. I bounced around for a couple of days until I ended up at my mom's apartment in Brentwood. But it wasn't long until it was out of control again. The manager and my mother would stand outside and try to dispel the crowds by telling people that I wasn't there. And even though I wanted them to go away, on the other hand, that was the way I supported my addiction.

So during the day, I started hanging out in the alleys doing business in the stucco-walled enclosures around dumpsters. They were great places to hide from the police, because we could shut the gates in front. We would also get in them to scavenge for clothes or anything that we could use or sell. In addition, we would also get high in the large cardboard dumpster that was behind a restaurant on the main street leading out of town. Some people were known to sleep together in there in addition to doing drugs.

However, at night, I would sneak people into the apartment. But every time, I opened the door, it squeaked. Soon Mom or my aunt caught on, and either one of them would come out and check. To solve that problem, I took the screens off and just had the people come through the windows.

There is no telling what the neighbors thought. I built a little hangout in the back porch to get high, and people would climb over the fence to party with me. I knew I had already pushed it passed the limit with the cops frequently coming around. The manager warned my mother, and the choices were easy. I would either get rid of all the drugs and have somewhere to stay or continue what I was doing and move. It made more sense to leave.

I tried staying away as much as I could, wandering the streets. It was a constant torment with the demons and voices. Sometimes, I could hear them so clearly. They were screaming. Sometimes they revealed themselves in the sound of cars crashing, gun fire, and explosions. There were sounds of people killing others and people being killed; sounds so awful that no visions would come to mind. Complete chaos, anarchy, and even the end of the world or a world without God. But what was I hearing? Why couldn't I see it?

I visited my mother and asked her, "Do you hear them? They are getting closer."

"What are you talking about?" she would ask.

"They are out there, and they are coming!" I shrieked.

I thought that at any moment they would be crashing through the windows and break down the door. I stood paralyzed, staring at the walls.

"I don't hear anything," my mother said.

I turned and looked into her eyes and yelled, "Are you in on it, Mom? Are you one of them? You know that you're not helping me by pretending they are not there!"

My mother was thinking about having me committed.

She hugged me and cried, "If the ambulance ever stops you and takes you away, it is only because I love you."

I said, "O.k. I'll see you later," like nothing happened.

My family called hospitals and different places to try and find help for me, but nobody could.

There was an old Catholic church that sat right in the middle of town, and sometimes, I would go sit on the pews, not to worship or to pray, but sometimes to question, sometimes to wonder, and sometimes to sleep. I would question God about why life has to be so full of misery? Why did I have to be born? Why do I feel so alone? I wondered what it would be like if I could be someone else. What if I was married, had children, and was in my right mind? What if I had a job and a home? I could sit there for hours and get lost in my thoughts. Ladies would come into the church with their rosaries and get on their knees, crawl to the front of the church, and pray.

I would watch them and think, "What could they possibly be doing or saying?"

One woman finished praying, got up, and began to walk towards the front door to leave. As she passed me, our eyes connected, and I realized that I had been getting high with her son for years.

I spent many days in the church, sometimes just to get away from the outside world. Life was never boring. There was always something going on. On the outside of the church, there was a little restroom. You could walk through a iron rod fence, pass by some statues, and the bathroom was right there. I used to think that demons lived in there, because one night, I sat down by the door and swore that there was somebody inside. I could hear whispering. I banged on the door and tried to pry open the window. I thought that I had captured some of the demons that were following me around. Depending on my behavior, people usually called the police on me, sometimes because I was acting weird or sometimes because I would argue, scream, and cuss at the top of my lungs at whoever was in there...or wasn't!

One time as I exited the church, I noticed police cars outside and cops standing with their guns drawn. I already knew the routine, so I came walking out with my hands up.

After they surrounded and questioned me, they got me down and stood around. I put my head down and began to cry. I wondered to myself when it was going to stop. I heard one of the officers calling my name, and as I looked up the street, a car was driving by very slowly. It just happened to be a lady whom had known my family for years. As she drove by, she stared out the window at me almost as if she could feel my pain. Again, the policeman called my name. I turned towards the officer, and to my surprise, it was one of my cousins. He had chosen to lead an honest life, and was never into drugs.

He asked me if I was o.k., but I did not answer him. He continued to ask questions, but I was so broken inside that all I could do was cry.

He asked, "What's wrong? How can I help you?"

There was so much going on with me that I didn't know where to start. All I could get out was, "I'm tired, and I want everything to stop!"

He talked to me for a few minutes, but since I didn't do anything to break the law, he had to let me go. Before I left, however, he asked me if I was hungry. He reached into his pocket and handed me some money. But I refused it and said that I was o.k. When does a dope fiend turn down free money?

It was years later when I was visiting my aunt that she began to tell a story about her son, the police officer.

She said that the cops were discussing their opinions of me and asked him his thoughts.

He said, "That's my cousin."

The officers laughed as if he was telling a joke.

"No, I'm serious," he told them. "He is my cousin. His mom and my mom are sisters."

I can only imagine their surprise finding out that he had a relative on the other side of the law.... way on the other side.

What My Sister Thought about Me

When I was about 22, there was a girl I knew who used to hitchhike in from a foothill town.

We'd be standing on Highway 4, a diesel would pull up, and she'd get out.

"We'd say, what are you doing here?"

She said, "Oh, I just hitchhiked here.

While here, she was usually with a group of men. She would be promiscuous, and then come to me to get high. I told her that she might as well get paid for sleeping with people and then she could get herself high.

Once, I took my more than willing friend to this man's house. I also took my little sister with me. While others would take their sister to the park or the mall, it was normal for me to take her places where I could hang out with people who were getting high and acting crazy. My sister saw the whole thing. Later in life, she told me that she would never forget that.

To my little sister, I was normal, and I was what a brother was like.

"I didn't think that you ever slept," she thought, "I just thought you were a machine."

I greatly regret all the horrible things that my sister saw, and how I had become.

I am sure that there are more terrible things that I cannot even remember. My mind was often so high on drugs or so foggy from my paranoia that I have no idea what I did or said. I'm sure that I have caused a lot a pain in the lives of others and that my influence for evil was great.

Alternative Lifestyle

All these years, I had been living a homosexual lifestyle behind closed doors. No one knew. I would never admit it to anyone, because I was afraid of what people might do to me.

Drugs really took me to a dark place. I would sleep with different men to get high. I didn't see sleeping with men for drugs as prostitution. I saw it as a free high. Sex didn't mean anything to me unless I was able to manipulate someone such as a non-gay man. I was sick.

When guys approached me in a sexual way, I thought it was a plot to kill me because of who I was. And even though I went along with it, I would always have something in hand like a needle, a nail, a piece of glass, anything that I could defend myself with if they did attack.

One time, this guy drove me all the way to a cornfield to sleep with him, but I stopped him because I saw and heard shadows and voices outside his vehicle.

I looked at him and questioned, "Did you bring me all the way out here to kill me?"

"Kill you?" he questioned. "What are you talking about?"

"I hear them outside the car. There they are!" I screamed as I pointed to the corn stalks. There's another one! And another one!"

I kept yelling, "Hurry up! They're going to kill me!

In a panic, I started tying to lock all the doors, and I cursed and screamed as loud as I could. I was hoping that someone would hear the commotion, but we were in the middle of a cornfield. Unsure of what to do, he asked me where I wanted him to take me. I could feel a presence all around me as if people were crawling around outside of the car. I don't know if there were really people out there or if they were demons. But either way, I did not want to be there.

It was two years after I left the garage that I met a guy who told me that I knew him before, but I didn't remember him. Through the years, I had met or known so many people that I didn't recall them all. Anyway, one night, he told me that some guys were trying to "get him".

"What do they look like?" I asked, He didn't know, but he said that he knew they were there.

"I have this place where we could stay," he suggested.

His plan was that one of us would sleep half the night, while the other would stay up and stand guard. And then, we would switch.

I agreed. So we walked for a half an hour and finally came to this field and an abandoned diesel trailer. It sat in the middle of the field. Ahead of it was the main highway to the left and a small shopping center to the right. As we climbed in from the back, I noticed junk everywhere.

Misinterpreting his intentions, I made advances towards him. The whole time, I thought it was a set-up. I thought he had lured me there so that people could jump me. After about thirty minutes, I began to think that I heard people walking around the trailer and talking. I figured that this was my cue to get out of there.

I remember that as I was leaving, he just sat there quiet and still. A few days later, I saw him walking down the street, and we started talking.

He asked, "Do you remember the other night in the field when you disrespected me?

I said, "Yes."

He then began to tell me that he was going to get a gun, put it to my head, and pull the trigger!"

I looked at him and just kind of smiled.

"Why are you smiling?" he inquired.

"Because I'm already dead!" I responded.

This man later became a Christian and is serving God.

There were always guys willing to do whatever I wanted in order to get a bag. It was in one of these situations that I met Partner #1. At first, I couldn't stand him and kept trying to get rid of him. But he kept coming back to the garage, smiling as usual. He wanted to be involved in this evil and corrupt world so badly.

After a few weeks went by, I got so tired of fighting with him that I said, "You know what? Whatever."

As I found out later, this guy was very intelligent. He knew what was good and what was junk. He was familiar with electronics and cars, and he was able to take things apart and put them back together. When I met him, he was getting ready to go to a school to learn how to become an airplane mechanic. He was "a square". Something about him was innocent and naïve. He was the first person that I let my guard down with, and as time went by, we became more and more involved. This relationship continued for about three years.

For the first time, everything was great, but the more I began to trust him and open up to him, the more addicted he became to the bag. It wasn't long afterwards that he began stealing and sleeping around. And if that wasn't enough, he got busted and told the cops everything they wanted to know about me. But because my self-esteem was so low, I thought that if I let him go, I would have no one. After that, things just got worse. I thought that we were in a partnership together, but he was in a relationship with my drugs. I believe what happened was that he began to get pressure from the guys who hung out outside and wanted to steal from me. They had turned against me, and little by little, he did, too. The relationship took a toll on both of us, and it brought us both to a place of constant fighting and rage. But I still wasn't willing to walk away. Then one day, he left. I used to stand outside of where we lived on the bottom of the hill. I would wait to see if his car would come over the hill, but it never did. I gave this relationship everything I had, the only way I knew how.

After about a month, I realized that he wasn't coming back. But in my business, people were coming in and out of my life everyday. It wasn't long before I met Partner #2. This partner really knew his game and said and did all the right things. He took the place of all my pain and emptiness. Soon, I began to see a pattern. This guy wasn't there for me; he, too, was there for the bag.

Partner #2 knew things about me that I couldn't even remember. He knew things about my tattoos that I didn't know or recall. He was more violent than the first. It was a weird relationship. One minute we could be fist fighting, throwing whatever we could get in our hands at each other, destroying furniture and burning each other's stuff. But the next moment, after we got tired, we would look at each other and start laughing at how crazy and out of control things got, and we would call a truce.

There were times when he wouldn't come home for days at a time and when I would confront him about it.

He would say, "What are you talking about?"

Things only got worse as time went by. Towards the end, he had absolutely no consideration for my feelings. One night, he came home with a girl and began to sleep with her right in front of me. I don't know if I felt more hurt, shocked, or confused. I knew in the past, he had been with a couple of guys, but this really had me messed up. One would think that this would have been the last straw, but it wasn't. Even with all the hurt, confusion, and anger, it was better than being alone. So I tried to hold onto the relationship for as long as I could. I was a human being, and I needed to know that somebody cared. I needed to know that I could be loved. It was like people came into my life playing this game, and as soon as I started playing it back, they didn't want to play anymore. In a weird way, I think what I was looking for in a man was for someone who would protect me, care about me, and do all the things my father was supposed to do and didn't.

Later, I learned from others that Partner #1 wasn't even gay. He just stayed in a relationship with me to get high.

Partner #2 had been missing in action for about a week, and I was tired of the game and ready for something new. But then one day, I looked up and who's standing in the doorway but Partner #1.

I let out a sigh of relief, looked twice, and said, "Is that you?"

"It's me", he said.

I felt as if I had been stranded on an island for a long time and was suddenly rescued. He stayed for a few days, then Partner #2 decided to come home. After introducing them to each other, they just kind of stared at each other. There was some obvious tension. Honestly, what they were both probably thinking was that I was their free ride, and that they didn't want the other one to take that away. We must have sat in the room for about two days getting high. The whole time, all I could think about was how to tell #2 that I didn't need him anymore without being mean. To my surprise, I didn't need to tell him. The two of them ended up leaving together!

After fighting with them both for months, I cut them off. However, both of them kept coming back and forth into my life. To get even with me, they even went as afar as to offer themselves to any guy that they thought I was talking to. Whenever they saw me talking to another man, they would go behind my back and approach that person, whether or not he was gay. Then, they would tell him things about me so that he would not want to see me again.

Partner #2 and I would fight, and then get together. In time, I learned that he was a mean man whose life was very dark. People used to tell me that he was the Devil and to just get rid of him.

When I told him that, he would laugh and say, "You're the Devil!"

After about a year of being with him, I said to him, "You know what? I'm done."

And I separated myself from him. But he didn't like that, and he started following me around. He would stalk me by hiding in the bushes, around the corner, in trees, and in cars. He liked to play mind games to make people feel like they were going crazy. Or maybe I was just crazy anyway. Well, I knew I was.

Number 2 had gotten involved with a girl who was into witchcraft. That is when my mind started to get even worse. I felt that they put some kind of curse or spell on me, because things just continued to get worse and worse. I knew more and more every day that I was losing my mind.

I remember sitting on some stairs one day holding my head repeating, "You're not going to take my mind!"

It is possible that I had more than one personality. I didn't have names for separate people, but I know that there was an innocent and helpful side of me, and on the other hand, there was a violent side, one with sex demons, and another consumed with drugs.

I was getting paranoid. I had thoughts that people were talking to me, following me (well, sometimes Partner # 2 stalked me), and threatening me. I tried to convince people that I wasn't nuts. One of the things that the demons liked doing was to tell all my secrets out loud. Because I heard them, I believed that everyone could. They were constantly trying to humiliate me to the point that I would start screaming back at them.

But I was talking to myself, screaming at my demons, because they were yelling at me. People would stare in unbelief. Some of them called the police.

Partner #2 also called the police, but he ratted me out so that he could get rid of me and get all of my business. I had taken him in and supported him, but I wasn't innocent. I had my part in all the madness, and in all that, I guess I just didn't care.

Months later, I had the feeling that someone was following me, so I went into the church. I originally thought that someone was trying to creep up behind me and kill me. I wanted to see if any of this suspicion would happen, and I must have fallen asleep. When I woke up, Partner #2 was sitting right behind me.

"I have been following you for days," he announced.

In my mind, all I could think was that he had come back to me. It had been a few months. We talked for a few hours, we got high, and then he said that he had to take care of something, but that he would be back.

I watched Partner #2 walk away. He got smaller and smaller; then he was gone, and all of a sudden I was alone again.

Chapter 5

The Months Became One Long Day

ഊ

Seven Against One

The cops wanted to run me out of town; people did not want me in their communities. I was completely lost. But even that wasn't enough to stop me from feeding my addiction.

My mother and my aunt moved to the house in Oakley with my uncle. This time, they allowed me to move back with them. People were not happy that I was coming back. I tried to hide as much as I could, but it only took one person to find out where I was. Soon, more and more people would come looking for me. Everyone assumed that I always had drugs on me. That was not true. I was using drugs, but at the time, I wasn't selling them. But that didn't stop people from wanting me to stay away. I knew that they wanted to keep the neighborhood free from any drugs at all.

One of the neighbors noticed all the traffic in front of the house and called the police. The officers said that they were keeping their eye on me. Somebody even went door to door telling everyone that there was drug dealing going on. With the help of the police department, some of the people started a neighborhood watch to make sure that I couldn't sell drugs. They invited everyone except us. Then, they put an ad in a local newspaper stating that I was a suspected drug dealer.

One of the reasons why some of the neighbors didn't want me around was because some of them were selling drugs and didn't want the attention around their houses. So what better way to throw people off than to be the ones working with the cops?

There was a cast iron fence around my uncle's house, and at night, he locked the gate. Everyone had gone camping except for my uncle, and he shut the gate. I was basically locked out. So, I climbed in his old car that hadn't run for a long time and had been parked on the street. Someone must have noticed I was sitting in the car and called some of his buddies. When I got out of the car, seven men, who were some of those who were trying to have me thrown out of the community, surrounded me and started pushing me around. I knew I was in trouble. I tried to push my way out of the circle to get closer to my uncle's house. I knew that there was a metal bar lying by the fence, but I wasn't able to reach it. It was then that I felt the smashing of what turned out to be a metal flashlight slamming against my face. At the same time, one of the guys was on the phone with the cops. Then, some others started getting in on the attack.

When the police came, they wanted to arrest me. Even though it was really an assault on me and they gave seven different stories, the police chose to believe them. I couldn't press charges on them, because it was their word against mine. They told me that there was nothing that I could do about it. I knew that my word wasn't worth much, so I just let it go as far as pressing charges. In my own mind, I knew that I had made my own bed and that I had to lay in it.

My uncle heard all the commotion and came outside to see what was going on.

I could imagine him thinking, "What now?"

After everything settled down, the police released me to my uncle, and we went inside. He went to bed, and I sat on the couch in the living room in the dark trying to figure out what just happened. I must have fallen asleep, because I remember waking up covered in blood. I must have bled all night from the open wound on my face. When I finally realized what was happening, I stood up and made my way to the bathroom to clean up. I was spewing blood wherever I went and what I touched….all over the walls, the furniture, everywhere.. The more I tired to clean up, the more mess I made. So I knew that I had to leave the house.

I left and walked down the street to a friend's house. She tried to help me get clean, but she couldn't because there was so much blood, which she described as like a pudding consistency. It took me about fifteen minutes with a water hose outside to wash all the blood off of me.

Later, when I talked to my uncle, he said that he wasn't aware of what had happened to me, and that is why he went to bed. He said that I had lost so much blood that night that it soaked through the couch and pooled underneath into a puddle on the carpet.

A few days later, my uncle received a letter saying that unless he threw me out, he would have to pay a fine to all the neighbors who signed the petition. So again, my mom and aunt packed what little they had left and moved away.

To show that the attack meant nothing to me, I went and stood in front of the house of one of the guys who attacked me. I stood there for a few hours talking to myself, just to entertain myself and to show him "nothing ventured, nothing gained."

Everywhere I went, the police would follow. They wanted me to stay out in the open so that they could keep an eye on me. Once behind walls, they wouldn't know if I was selling or not. If I went to a house, the police would go there and tell the renters that there was drug activity when I was around, and if they didn't get me to leave, they could evict everyone. They would then call the owners of the house to tell them it could be seized if there was drug dealing going on. People would want me to leave for fear of being evicted, and if they were doing drugs themselves, they didn't want the police there to find out. In the eyes of the police, anyone around me was guilty by association.

When I was in the garage in Oakley, the police would watch me for hours. They may have thought that I was some kind of drug ringleader, because they said that a lot of people on the streets who were busted for drugs gave my name. But in reality, I wasn't a drug ringleader. I was just an addict running as fast and as hard as I could from the real world.

Before we were evicted from the apartment in Brentwood, the police told me that they knew that I had continually escaped arrest, but that some way or another, I would slip up and they would get me. It just seemed that everywhere I stepped, a bomb was going to go off, just like in a minefield. One wrong move and everything would come crumbling down. I know the things I was doing were wrong, but I really didn't know anything else. Remember, I was running not only from the law and life, but from myself.

Before leaving the apartment in Brentwood, I had found a ride to meet a connection. We were supposed to meet at a parking lot in town. It was late at night, and I knew that this might be the last opportunity to score some D that day. We were still on the road and when we arrived at a store, I noticed her car backing up. I panicked and began to get out of the car while we were still moving. Without thinking, I opened the door and put my foot on the road. Then, I heard something crack. The car stopped, and I limped over to the connection.

She asked, "Why are you limping?"

"I thought you were driving away," I replied.

"No! I was just parking," she said.

We did our business exchange, and I got dropped off at my mother's apartment. My foot was in excruciating pain, but I figured that I would just work the pain out as I did many times before. I got high and started off on my nightly walk. I got about two blocks and realized that the pain was getting worse. But I kept walking until it was unbearable. I threw myself to the sidewalk and began dragging myself.

I yelled, "Help! Help!"

But no one responded. Then, I screamed as loud as I could. I was lying in front of a movie theater. On one side there were restaurants and businesses. On the other side and a block down was a residential section. A car drove past me very slowly. Someone in that car may have seen that it was me, because they drove off. Some people stood outside of their houses and were watching me as I yelled out for their help. They just turned away and went back into their homes. After about thirty minutes, a lady went to my mom's and told her that her son was lying in the middle of the street

The lady told her that she had talked to some other neighbors and they had said, "Oh, he's o.k. He's just crazy. He always acts like that."

But the lady thought I was really in trouble. Mom didn't wait for her to finish. She just began running and looking for me. By the time she got to where I was, a police officer had pulled up and put me in his car. He drove us back to the apartment. After we arrived, I began to cry. I thought to myself that if I were dying, nobody would have helped me. Nobody would have cared. And the pain of my broken heart surpassed the pain in my foot.

Although I often found places to stay, there were other times when I just sat on benches, hid in bushes or trees, or just walked along the road.

I was a mess. Filthy. Ragged. Unsightly. My toenails grew so long that they would rip through my socks and cut into my toes. The skin on my feet was so dry that it would pull off, and I would lose the top layer. Every time I stepped, the nails in my boot would stab into my feet. It hurt to walk. Because of the pain, I sometimes walked like a decrepit monster. I am sure that I was very scary looking.

I would spend the night in porta potties, or in the bushes or bathrooms in the park near a middle school.

Once in downtown Oakley, I pointed something out, "See that bench over there? That was my home for a while. I just stayed there."

When asked if I had a blanket to cover me at night, I replied, "No, I just sat there on the bench."

I also said, "Do you know those oleander bushes on side of the road coming into Brentwood? I slept in there, too. I was completely hidden. If you ever hear noises in the bushes, it very well could be a homeless, drug addict living in there. People would be surprised where the homeless hang out. I became like a lost dog sleeping outside on the ground and eating whatever I could find.

"I also spent a lot of time in a big tree near the old railroad tracks that went through a main part of town. When the tree was at its fullest, we would climb up in the branches and get high. It was known as "The Party Tree."

One time before I lived in the garage and was looking for a place to stay, I broke into an abandoned hearse in a backyard. When I got into it, I accidentally locked the doors. All my paranoia and fears built up in me, and I panicked. I honestly believed that I was locked in with a demon. I punched out the window and kicked the door. Then, it opened...which it would have done anyway if I had pressed the unlock button, and I walked out like nothing had happened.

Little by little, I was pushed out of different communities, and I usually stayed along the highway. Sometimes, I would sit on the side of the road near a neighborhood of houses. There would be kids playing, laughing, and having a good time like children should. One time when I was sitting down on the side of a street, a woman came out of one of the homes and started yelling at her kids. She was just making sure that they didn't get in trouble, and she repeated herself a few times.

Then, in her last attempt to control her children, she pointed to me and yelled, "If you kids don't listen, I'm going to let that monster take you!"

The children started screaming and yelling "Monster!" "Monster!" as they ran in different directions trying to get away from me.

My heart melted. It was like someone was throwing gasoline on the fire or salt on an open wound. I stood up as quickly as I could and walked away hurt, embarrassed, and ashamed.

"Doesn't the world know that I am a human and that I have feelings?" I asked myself.

Life on the streets was agonizing. It was like it's own kind of prison. Minutes turned into hours, hours turned into days, days, turned into weeks, and weeks turned into years. Life was like one long day. Sometimes, it was day; sometimes, it was night. Sometimes, it was hot; sometimes, it was cold. Most of the people I knew kind of wrote me off. I had lost the ability to determine what voices were real…the ones coming from people… from the ones I heard in my head.

I remember waking up on the side of the road during the winter. I didn't own a watch, but I could tell approximate time by what was going on and how dark it was. It must have been about 3:00 a.m., because there were no cars out and it was completely dark. As I stood, I noticed that I was covered in ice. Every bone in my body snapped as I began to walk. The wind and rain hit my skin, and it felt like fire. I knew that if I wanted to warm up, I would have to start moving. I could hardly walk, but I put one foot in front of the other with very slow and agonizing steps and continued to do so. The demons were walking right next to me, yelling and cussing at me. I am sure they were angry because they were hoping that I would have continued sleeping and eventually would have died of hypothermia. I was living in such a dark world that I never was able to see the blessings of God like waking me up just in time so that I didn't freeze to death.

Sometimes I would look up at the sky and thought I saw God looking down at me, pointing and laughing at my pain and suffering.

I thought that God joked, "Ha," Ha" over and over.

I would respond, "Now kill me and put me out of my misery!"

Other times, I would just sit and watch people go by. While sitting there, it felt like maggots were eating and living in my brain.

I would also sit and watch people as they drove past in their cars, and depending on the expression on their faces or how they were dressed, I would make up little stories about their lives. Maybe it thought they were going to a party or a wedding, or maybe they were fighting or mad at each other. Sometimes, if they were sitting close to each other, I would think of their happy lives.

If I would be walking past a residential neighborhood, I would try to imagine what was going on. For instance, one day I was walking and across the street, a car pulled up into the driveway. Three little kids jumped out yelling and screaming like kids do without a worry in the world. The mother got out and reminded them to make sure that they get their book bags out and then followed them up to the door.

The car alarm clicked off, and they all paraded into the house. One by one, they entered the house. The front door shut, and it was silent. It was a good neighborhood, and the house was nice. The children all seemed to be dressed very well, and I assumed they were well disciplined and the house was in order. I tried to imagine what they were doing inside.

I guessed that maybe the mom was encouraging the kids to start their homework. Then, I pictured her going through the mail and checking her messages on the phone. I sat down on the sidewalk and got comfortable. I was lost in my own thoughts. After a few hours went by, I imagined that the kids were sitting in the living room watching cartoons and playing while the mother prepared dinner.

Sometime afterwards, a second car pulled up, and as the man got out of his car, the kids came running out yelling, "Daddy", "Daddy".

The man took the time to hug each one before they entered the house and shut the door. Then, it was quiet again. I sure wish that my father would have hugged me like that.

I imagined that the man spent some time with his kids while he talked to his wife. And they shared about how each other's day went. I pictured them as they sat around the dinner table. They had plenty of good food. And everyone had smiles on their faces. As the sun went down, the lights went on. I thought that after the long day, they all settled down in the living room and cuddled up together on the couch watching t.v. One by one, the kids began to fall asleep, and later, throughout the house, the lights went off. I imagined that they were snuggled up in their beds. I thought to myself that it must be nice to know that when you are tired, you have somewhere to sleep. When you are hungry, you have something to eat. And when you go somewhere, you have a house to come home to. I sat there and reflected on how lucky these people were.

The next morning, I realized that I must have fallen asleep in my thoughts and had been there overnight. It had been raining all night. A different man approached me. I was wet and cold, lost and confused. The man walked right up to me. I thought he was going to saying something to the effect that I couldn't sit there. But instead, he handed me a cup of coffee and a donut and a napkin. As our eyes met, he put the food in my hands.

It was almost as if his eyes were saying, "I don't know how I can help you."

I quickly looked away from him out of shame and embarrassment. He turned, got into his car, and drove away. It made me think that the same way I was watching the other family, somebody was studying me.

The coffee was hot, and the donut looked fresh. And I was starving. I stared at them for about twenty minutes. Then the demons began speaking saying that it was all a trick and that the man poisoned the coffee because he didn't want me to sit on his lawn. Suddenly, thoughts about how he may have tampered with the breakfast rushed through my mind. I reached over and set the food in a flow of water and watched it all wash away in the rainwater and sludge.

As I walked away, I asked myself, "Yeh, right. Why would anyone want to be nice to me?"

What had just happened was rare. But every once in a while, people would reach out to me with compassion. They would approach me and hand me money or a jacket. I would stare at their faces, and without responding, I would get up and walk away. There was a guy who pulled up to where I was sitting next to a building. He got out of this car, approached me, and tried to speak to me.

He reached out his hand and said, "Here. You can buy something to eat."

I just stared at him as he stood with a hand full of money.

I turned away and snapped, "I don't need your money, and I don't want your help!"

I lay down and curled into a ball trying to keep myself warm as he stood there a few seconds. Later, he walked away. He sat in his car, then returned after a few seconds taking off his jacket.

"Here. Take my jacket then. It's cold out here and you're going to freeze to death," he insisted.

I looked at him once again and saw the frustration on his face. He wanted so bad to help me, but the demons controlling me wouldn't let him.

He finally left, and I thought to myself, "Doesn't he understand? I'm hopeless!"

Well, I shouldn't have thought hopeless, because I knew in my mind that life isn't forever. Sooner or later, I was going to have to die. Then, this whole hellish, nightmare life would be over.

Another time, I remember that it was Christmas Eve. It was late, and I was walking on the street when a truck pulled over. The driver began to tell me that his older brother knew one of my cousins. He then told me that he just left his mother's house and that they were making tamales.

He held out this paper sack and said, "Here. Take as many as you want."

I was starving, but embarrassed. I reached in and grabbed one.

"Come on. Take some more. Put some in your pocket for later," he insisted.

He began to tell me that he was a Christian and that he lived on the next street over. He also said that if I ever wanted to talk or if I just wanted to sleep, he had a nice warm couch.

I said, "O.K.," and he drove off.

I quickly sat down and enjoyed the tamales. A Christian man had just brought me my Christmas dinner, and although grateful, I didn't express it. In fact, I was uncomfortable about the whole situation. I was often so busy with the demons and voices that I didn't have time for reality. I mostly just walked back and forth between Oakley and Brentwood. I didn't understand it at the time, but now I realize that I was also dealing with territorial demons on top of the ones inside me. As I walked down the highway, I would come to certain areas where the demons were more aggressive than other parts of the road. Mostly, the evil spirits would laugh at me and call me names. But every once in a while, one would approach like a rabid beast to let me know that this area was taken. In my own weird way, I fought and argued back with the spirits. I couldn't always see them, but I could hear them and I could certainly feel their presence. There were times at night that I would see someone walking towards me. I wasn't sure if it was a human or a demon.

Sometimes, I would run towards it and scream, "Kill me! Kill me!"

But other times, I would contort my body and moan or hiss. Then I would walk backwards in slow motion like a very old person. And sometimes, I would get on the ground and drag myself. I was afraid that I didn't know what to do. I think about it now and then. It must have been horrifying to watch. I can imagine that if anyone happened to cross my path at night, they would never forget what they saw. This went on for many years.

Walking down the street, one minute I would talk to God, and the next minute I would be speak to Satan. I would be a prostitute; then I would be a scared little boy and on and on all within about ten minutes. There were times I would wear make-up and resemble a woman, but at the same time, I would look like a beast. When approached by people, I became very uncomfortable because of my physical appearance, the way I smelled, and how dirty I was. I tried to stay away from crowds, so I cut through the fields or back roads to avoid contact with anyone.

I didn't matter whether it was summer or winter; my clothes were old and ragged, because I kept wearing whatever I owned. If I had needed anything new, rather new to me, I could always find something in the dumpster or thrown by the side of the road. But I couldn't leave my belongings anywhere, because the minute you leave something somewhere, you lose it. So, I kept wearing what I owned. Summers were hot as I walked around with a long, black leather jacket. But at night, my jacket doubled as a blanket or sometimes a pillow. At times, I would bury myself in my jacket and pull my hood over my head to block out the world. The ground was my bed, and I usually used my fists as a pillow. The sky was my blanket. For entertainment or t.v., I just watched my surroundings. To change the channel, I would walk to another place and continue my viewing.

I would be so hungry that I would force myself to fall asleep so I didn't have to feel the pain in my stomach. Then I would wake up in the morning, only to feel that pain again. I was so tired. Hunger had a lot to do with it. The fight inside was gone. The will to live was gone. I looked like a walking corpse, empty and willing to die. Sometimes I told Satan that if he would give me the desires of my heart, I would help destroy as many lives as he wanted me to, and in the end, they would burn in hell, as would I. I felt that would make God angry. Because I believed I was nothing, it didn't surprise me that the Devil didn't want me either. Why would he? That went on for some time. Today, I realize that Satan's promises are empty and powerless.

My aunt would drive my mother up and down the highway because they knew that sooner or later, they would either find me walking along somewhere or at worst, dead in a ditch.

I would always keep my eye open for my aunt's car. There were a few times that I saw her vehicle and chased after it, but I wasn't quick enough and would watch it as it disappeared down the lonely street. I knew that this might be the only time that I could eat that week, and it was a time to relax and feel safe. Sometimes while in the car, my aunt would drive and play the radio. Mom would hold me, and I would sleep. Then, they would drop me off again. I had put them in jeopardy so many times before; I wasn't allowed to stay where they lived. The only way that people would open their door to my mother was if I wasn't with her.

That was my relationship with my mother for a long time. She would cry and plead with me to stop, saying that she loved me, but it was like she was talking in a different language. I would just walk away. It was easy for people to say the word "STOP", but only God, the Devil, and I knew what kind of war was going on in my head.

A local policeman once told me that the Brentwood Police Department had more calls on me in one night that any other person in town all year! I have a page of recorded incidents with their department and who knows how many with the Office of the Sheriff. In reading them over, I could not remember them all.

After a few years, people knew me as the crazy man who lived on the side of the road.

I remember turning around in circles one day next to the highway asking myself, "What have I done to myself? How did I get here?"

I had really lost grips with reality. I was paranoid and thought people were out to kill me. I thought there were animals and insects that were eating me from the inside out. I was so consumed with this fear that I would have to go into the bushes, find and sharpen sticks, glass, and nails against the road, then, cut and poke myself so that the animals or bugs could get out. That was the only way I could get it to stop. I had holes in my face and my arms. In addition to holes I had dug, one could follow a path on my arms and hands where my veins had collapsed from years of shooting up.

I would also hit myself with sticks and scream, "Get them off of me!" as I felt the animals were also crawling on me. Even other drug addicts and homeless people were embarrassed to be around me.

I remember telling God, "What did I ever do to you to make you hate me so much? I never asked to be born. If you wanted to save me, you could. If you cared anything about me, you would at least kill me and put me out of misery."

"God, I want to die! I can't live like this anymore," I insisted. "I'm not strong enough to fight this battle, even if you send me to hell, just release me from this body that I'm living in"

I then threw myself down on the ground and cried myself to sleep in the pouring rain.

The months became one long day.

Chapter 6

And Then...

ꙮ

"Drive By"

There was one time I was sitting at my sister's home with my mom. Neither one of us spoke for twenty minutes. We really didn't have anything to say. I imagine she was just as exhausted as I was. My mother left the room, and I stood up and walked towards the door. I opened it, walked out, and shut it. When I heard the door close, something clicked in my head.

Voices cried, "KILL YOURSELF".

And that is what I wanted to do. I was in my early thirties, and I was so low and so depressed that I thought that was the only thing that I could do. I knew it was time. So I walked outdoors and started walking down the street towards the highway. The voices in my head convinced me to throw myself in front of a diesel truck.

I remember the voices saying, "If you throw yourself in front of the diesel, it will only hurt for a second. Then it will be all over."

In reality, all I wanted was for the pain to stop. No more waiting for God to kill me. But what I didn't know was that there were other plans for my life and that He would use a lady who saw me walking along the road to talk to me.

"I saw him everywhere," a lady I will call "Mary" said. "The Lord must have put him in the places I was going, because I kept seeing him around town."

It was uncanny! She would see me in town, out of town, and walking along the highway or other streets on her way to where she was going. Sometimes, after she ran various errands, I would show up ahead of her on the way back!

One time, she was driving down a few streets towards the highway, when she saw me standing by a house. It was my sister's house, and my mom lived there, too.

Some time later, Mary went to that house and knocked on the door. She had no idea if the people in the house knew me or not, but she was determined to be obedient. She explained to my mother that she was looking for this guy whom she had seen walking along the street and that she had seen him in front of this house.

Mary explained, "The Lord has been leading me to find him and to pray for him. But I don't know who he is. Do you know him?"

My mother responded, "That is my son, and he lives on the streets. He's so far gone that we don't know how to reach him anymore."

Mary even had a dream that she shared God with someone who was severely bleeding and was going to die. I now believe that the dream was about me.

She prayed, "Lord, if you want me to talk to him, let me know."

I was about fifty steps from the highway, and I was getting pumped up to run out onto the street and in front of a diesel, when suddenly, a white Chrysler drove by and made a U-turn. My first thought was that somebody was coming to kick me down one last time! The car pulled over and someone rolled down the window. There was a lady driving with a little girl in the front seat.

The lady said, “Excuse me sir, but did you know that God loves you more than you can ever imagine?”

I looked at her and yelled, “God doesn’t love me; I’d rather be on fire!”

She said that everywhere she went, she saw me and that she told her husband that the Lord must want her to pray for me.

He husband had told her that if she ever stopped and talked to me to make sure that he was with her, because I looked crazy and I might try to attack her.

But she said that as she drove by, the Lord spoke to her saying that if she didn’t talk to me now, tomorrow would be too late.

That is when I knew that God was talking to me, because I knew that what she said was true. I was just about to throw myself in front of the first truck I saw. How did she know? Why did I stop from committing suicide?

That day, Satan failed again from accomplishing his mission.

She prayed, and then she told me, “The same way that I see you walking up and down these streets day and night doing whatever you are doing, I see you one day walking with a Bible in your hands, preaching the Word of God.”

“Yeh, right,” I thought to myself.

It was strange to me, because she acted like I was a movie star or someone important, and yet, the people who I grew up with or knew for a long time would turn away when they drove past me. She would go out of her way to pull over, and she wanted me to meet her family. I was ashamed and embarrassed, because I was dirty and I smelled. I just kind of looked at them in the car. I didn’t want to speak, because most of my teeth were rotted out.

For the first couple of months, she'd see me on the street, stop, and say, "God loves you. Are you ready, yet?" (meaning, "Was I ready to accept Jesus as my Savior and follow Him?").

I'd say, "No", and walk away.

I was thinking, "What kind of lady would bring her family to meet me?"

Things didn't change for the next year. I continued to live on the streets, use drugs, and it even seemed like the war inside of me got even more intense.

One time, Mary came to my sister's house and knocked on the door.

My mother answered, and she said, "I am looking for Eli. God has put it on my heart to pray for him."

Then she left a message for me with my mom. The message was that she was going to pray for me every Friday at 3:00 p.m. for one hour. In addition, I was invited to come and talk with her and pray. But even if I didn't come there, she would still pray.

I did go to her house, and she talked to me about the Lord, and prayed. And I came back over and over, sometimes because I was trying to figure out what was going on in my life, sometimes for free food, and sometimes just to get away from the world. But there were times that I didn't go. And she still prayed. Eventually, I quit going, but Mary continued to pray. She prayed that I would stop my destructive lifestyle and turn to the Lord. She asked that God would start pulling away everything in my life that was pulling me down, and that when I did drugs, I would not get the high I wanted. She prayed that all the evil in my life would come to an end.

After that, things got even worse.

Shot At

I was standing on the corner of Highway 4 and Hill Avenue, a place where I stood a lot, when a car drove by very close, about three feet or so away, and stopped at the stop sign. I saw an arm stick out the window and then I heard, "Blat!", "Blat!" Whoever it was shot again. Then the car drove off. It happened so quickly that all I could do was look at the bullet holes in the car behind me. I never found out who the shooter was or why. I started yelling and cussing at the car. Soon a police car came up, and the officer wanted to arrest me. I told him that I had just been shot at, but since I didn't know who it was or why, he just told me to get off of the street. The policemen didn't really know what to make of me, my different personalities, and my psychotic behavior.

Another time, it was 1:00 a.m., and I was walking on my street. Out of nowhere, three cars drove past me and down the street. Then they made U turns and faced me. Two cars sped towards me and passed me, and the third stayed there like in a stand off. In the next split second, a shot was fired. Whoever it was shot again. It happened so fast that there was no time to think. And then, I heard a third shot and the whistle of a bullet that flew past me and embedded in the telephone pole that was next to me. I didn't know whether or not I was hit. But amazingly, I was spared.

In both cases, the shooters were close enough, but "somehow" and for "some reason", they did not hit me.

When the suggestion was made to me that I dig the casing out of the telephone pole as a souvenir, I said, "Oh, that's o.k. There are lots of souvenirs I could get along the highway, mostly syringes."

Since I spent most of the time walking along the road, I never knew if cars would drive by and shoot at me or if they would run me over. One of the battles that I fought every day was that I wanted to die, but at the same time, I was afraid to kill myself.

The Hammer Attack

Once, I was sitting on the side of a street playing with a knife. I was so paranoid that I always tried to have a knife, metal pipe, or a hammer with me, but not a gun. Yet, it was hard for me to carry a weapon, because I never knew when the cops would search me. They had warned me that if they ever saw one in my hand, they would arrest me. So, I tried to hide these things from them. The policemen really didn't need a reason to stop and search me. I was always suspicious and had built a reputation of being no good. Sometimes, they would drive right past me and pay me no mind. But other times, I would get stopped, over and over. They were looking for any reason to lock me up and get me off the streets. But I avoided that at all costs, because going to jail would only put a wedge between my addiction and me.

It was night, and I was in front of a small local bar on the highway in Oakley. When a policeman drove by, I pushed the knife that I was carrying into the ground because I was afraid that he would return to search me. While this was going through my mind, I heard the sound of footsteps rushing towards me from behind. By the time I could turn around to see what it was, I felt a heavy blow to my head. It happened so quickly that the next thing I realized was that I was being kicked in the ribs on both sides and that there was another person standing over me who was hitting me on the head with what felt like and was a hammer.

I remember wondering, "How many times can you get hit in the head before you die?"

It seemed like an eternity, but it was probably only minutes or seconds before they quit. What probably stopped them was that people started to gather. But they didn't intervene; they just stood there and watched. Soon, the attackers ran back to their vehicle and drove off. I must have had a lot of survival adrenaline in me at the time, because I jumped up and chased the vehicle as it drove off. That was certainly a foolish thing to do, but again, not much of what I did made any sense.

Then, I stopped, stood there in a daze, and asked myself, "Why am I so wet?"

I felt like someone had poured a pitcher of water over me. It was then that I realized that I was bleeding from my head and that it wouldn't quit.

When I went back to the people who were standing and watching, not wanting to get involved, they just said, "Oh, you're all right."

But I knew that I wasn't. I was covered in blood, and there was no sign of it stopping. I remembered that I had a friend who had just gotten out of prison after being locked up for four years, and he only lived a couple blocks down. For purposes of this book, his name will be "Paul".

I had known Paul for years. In fact, he stayed with me when I lived in the garage. When he went to prison, I had money, a home, and I was at the top of my game. But years later when he got out, things were different. I was standing on the roadside when he saw me.

I was homeless; he could tell by looking at me. But I was too ashamed to tell him.

"I always see you walking on the highway. Where do you live?" he asked.

He told me where he lived and remarked, "If you ever get hungry, come to my house and I will feed you."

A few days went by, and I took Paul up on his offer. I went to his house and hoped that he would ask me if I was hungry. And he did. In fact, he reminded me how I helped him before he went to prison and that now he wanted to return the favor. He then asked me to move in with him, his girlfriend, daughter, and soon to be son.

I stumbled along to his house and banged on his front door. Each time I knocked, I splashed blood on the door.

He came out, trying to figure out what was going on.

Shocked, he asked, "What happened?" "What happened?"

I recapped what had happened to me, and he dragged me to his truck and headed towards the hospital. I can remember that all I wanted to do was to sleep. But he kept yelling at me to wake up. It was getting harder and harder to breathe, so I started to think that the only thing I could do was to roll down the window and jump out; I figured that I could breathe better outside. I could feel Paul pulling me back in the vehicle; he was trying to drive with one foot and one hand while he reached over and tried to restrain me from throwing myself out of the window. He then held me on the floorboard of the passenger side with his other foot and hand. I don't know how he did it, but he kept me from jumping out.

At one point, I recall almost blacking out. Paul yelled at me to wake up and breathe. I began to panic, because I thought I was dying. But throughout the whole ordeal, Paul stayed calm.

I thought that I wasn't going to live long enough to make it to the hospital, so I told him to take me to a lady that I knew.

"She's a nurse!" I cried. "She can help me!"

When we got there, the nurse yelled, "Oh, no! I can't help you. You need to go to the emergency room; your head is split wide open and hanging over!"

And she quickly called 911. I could see in her eyes that she knew it was worse than I had thought.

Then, I remembered that Mary "just happened" to live about seven houses away.

I told Paul, "Leave me right here and quick run down the street about six or seven houses and just scream Mary's name until she comes out of her house. When she comes out, bring her to me and tell her that I'm dying."

I just sat where I was in a lady's front yard sort of like a fountain. But instead of a beautiful statue with water running out of it, I was a beaten up body with blood running down my face and shoulders.

Mary "just happened" to being having a Bible study at the time. Paul didn't know her, but he began yelling, "Mary, Mary!"

She quickly came out of her house. Paul told her what had happened, and they both ran back to me. The police were there with the paramedics and the ambulance. It had been a good forty-five minutes since I was jumped.

Paul wanted to keep a low profile because he was on parole. But he never left my side except for when he went to get Mary.

Mary prayed for me out there in the lawn. I was the wounded, bleeding man who was in her dream. She was obedient to God when He told her talk to the wild, crazy man who was about to kill himself. Her obedience to God in talking to me at that moment in time, and not a minute too soon, made it possible for me to meet her and to later come to her house like a wounded bird and receive more prayers towards my complete recovery. God had orchestrated all of this. At the same time that the Devil was talking to me, Mary was praying for me.

When I arrived at the hospital, my sister had already been informed about the beating and was waiting for me in a room. I remember that they put me in this room, and I could hear the doctors talking in muffled voices. They were saying that they couldn't stop the bleeding. There was a doctor sitting on top of me, pushing my head back into place, while another one behind me sewed it together.

Mary and her husband, my sister, Paul and his girlfriend came to the hospital to see me a little later that night to make sure I was o.k. They had a church service and prayed for me in the waiting room.

I remember my sister pleading with me. She asked, "Will you please stop now?"

"Stop what?" I thought.

But I really knew what she meant. I needed to stop living my destructive lifestyle. But after going through all that I went through, that was all I knew. This was just an ordinary day in the life of an addict. This was reality.

I remember waking up the next morning. I was numb, but sore. The nurse told me that I was free to go. After Paul had left the hospital, his girlfriend went into labor. So he rushed her to a different hospital. Later, she gave birth to the baby boy. On his way back from being with them, Paul decided to stop by my hospital to check up on me. I was sitting outside in a wheelchair wondering what to do next. Just then, Paul pulled up. I was still in my hospital gown and covered with blood. My head was bandaged and stained.

I got into his truck, and he took off his sweater and said, "Here, put this on."

Paul kind of smiled and said, "I thought you were dead. I have seen people get jumped and shot, but I have never seen that much blood come out of one person before."

In my weakened state, I asked him if he had a hammer. I told him that I wanted to be ready the next time if someone tried to attack again. He gave me a hammer, and after arriving back at his house, I walked back to the same spot where the attack took place.

People were driving by slowly and staring at me. It didn't occur to me that they had slowed down to look at this crazy man in a hospital gown who was covered with red stains with a blood-soaked bandage around his head. But I thought they were the ones who had attacked me and that they were going to beat me up again. Being as paranoid as I was, I started chasing one of the cars with the hammer. Can you imagine how scary that must have been for them? I'm sure that I provided enough nightmares for those people for a long time!

For the next two months, Paul took care of me like a brother. He took me into his home and treated me like family. Paul was well respected on the streets and in prison, and he was a wonderful friend to me. Well, he was more than a friend; he was like an angel.

Back when we were both staying in the garage, I felt that not only were animals eating me from the inside out, but they lived in the furniture and that they were trying to get out to attack. Every time I sat in a chair or on a couch, I felt that it moved and that it was because of an animal. So I continually got up in the middle of the night, got a sledgehammer, and started breaking the furniture into pieces. Instead of criticizing me, Paul understood. He didn't say anything, but he went over, picked up another hammer, and started smashing things, too. Once we finished, we sat on a pile of the rubbish that was once furniture.

Paul laughed and asked, "Well, did you find what you were looking for?"

I replied, "No, they must have gotten away!"

While recovering from my injuries at Paul's, never once did the party stop. Nothing really changed. Paul had a job, but he didn't feel comfortable leaving me at his house. So he took me to "Terry's" house. She was a girl that we had known for a long time, and we all went though so much together. So during the day, I stayed at her home. And then later, Paul would pick me up and take me back to his house.

I wasn't fully recovered from my injuries from the day before, but after Paul dropped me off, Terry and I went over to the neighbor's so that we could get high. I remember trying to hit the pipe and falling over on my face. Then I threw up. As I lay face down in my vomit, everyone looked at me and didn't know what to do. I felt so helpless, everyone got up and left the room. Then, Terry came over and helped me up.

One morning when Paul took me to Terry's, we walked in and noticed that her house was covered in blood and that she sat in her room by herself.

Apparently, she had been cut the night before. I didn't know what she was going through, but before Paul left for work, he gave her some crank and a pipe so that she could get high while I cleaned up the blood all over the house. We didn't question her about what happened. We kind of knew and understood.

Paul knew more about me that I thought he did. He once told me about a man who lived with him and his dad in the past. The man was gay, and Paul told him that if he ever tried to touch him or anything, he would kill him. That was Paul's way of telling me not to be confused about why he was helping me.

The thing about Paul was that he just got out of prison, and he was trying to change his life. He had a good job and a new family. I asked myself why he would want to risk everything he was doing for someone like me? He knew I was trouble, but he saw past all that. At one point after getting me out of the hospital, Paul even fed me with a spoon because I was unable to feed myself. But as soon as I could, I started to look for a way to get high and to survive.

Paul didn't want to take any chances with druggies. He said that he wouldn't feel that his family was safe when he went to work if these people came looking for me. So he told me that some strange guys were out to get me. He then rented another house across town and said that we were moving. He told me about a job that he had out of town with his uncle and that he wanted to take me with him. He wanted me to start over with a brand new life, and he wanted to be a part of helping me finding it. He said that we could have normal lives. No more drugs. No more chaos. And it would be a new beginning. Paul said that we deserved a better life than the one we were living. But neither one of us had the chance to find out.

Soon after, Paul became ill. He was taken to the hospital, and he died the next day. I don't know why. I never saw Paul again.

His passing really confused me. I started to believe that I was a curse and that everywhere I went, people were throwing me out, losing their homes, and even dying. I ended up back on the streets.

A few months went by, and my mother and sister moved again. I had no idea where.

One day, I was walking and a guy that I had known for years stopped and asked, "What are you doing?"

I told him that I was trying to get to my mother's house.

He replied, "Get in; I'll take you."

After driving in circles for about three hours, he asked, "Where are we going? Tell me where your mother lives so that I can take you there."

I responded, "I don't know where she lives. I thought you knew and that was why you said you would give me a ride."

He stopped his car and looked at me confused. I opened the door and walked away. It was about two or three in the morning, and I saw this guy stealing gas out of a car. He stopped me and tried to explain what he was doing and that he had permission. I told him that I didn't care and that it was none of my business. After he got the gas and put it in his truck, he asked me if I needed a ride.

I replied, "I'm not going anywhere, but if you want to get high, I have some D."

He said "o.k." We parked and got high. I thought that I could persuade him to sleep with me. For some reason, I thought that if a man was nice to me that maybe he liked me, and my mind would make up a fantasy relationship. It was like the demons would start to manifest, and, of course, I was their slave. I had to do whatever I could to satisfy them, and if I couldn't please them, I would have had to pay a price. Sometimes, I could feel the demons touching me sexually. Then, I would roam the streets trying to find someone to sleep with. If I couldn't, I felt tormented to the point of wanting to commit suicide.

After sitting in the truck a few hours, he told me about his life. Basically, he lived in his vehicle, and his family moved away. After making the first move, I noticed that he was not interested. I had to be careful because I never knew what the other person might do. It could go either way. They could go along with it or, on the other hand, they might kill me.

There were times when I got myself into situations where I would ask, "Why do I keep doing this to myself?"

A few days went by, and a truck pulled up.

"Hey, do you need a ride?" the driver asked. It was the same guy.

"I'm not really going anywhere," I answered.

"That's o.k. Get in," he replied.

I thought to myself that this guy knows what I'm about, so it is all good."

We drove around for a while, parked and got high, but nothing happened. This went on for a few weeks.

"What do you want from me?" I finally asked. "Why do you keep picking me up and playing these little games?"

"I just want to be your friend," he said.

"You know what? I don't need any friends!" I snapped and started to get out of the truck.

"Wait!" he interrupted. "I know some guys out of town that want to buy some drugs."

I told them about you, and they said to bring you by.

I said, "Let's go!"

We started driving. We must have been on the road about two hours when we pulled up outside of a house.

He told me, "Hold on, and I will be right back.

I thought I heard people talking about killing me and making comments and threats against homosexuality. I started to realize that this was a set up.

When he came back to the truck, he said, "All right, they're ready for you."

I yelled, "Get in real quick!"

As I searched for a weapon, I found a large screwdriver. I pushed it towards him, and said, "Start the truck!"

"What are you talking about?" he asked.

"I know you guys are going to try to kill me. Start the truck!" I screamed. "I am going to stab the first person who approaches this vehicle, and if you don't drive, you'll be the first!"

And we drove off. We went in circles. He insisted that we park, but I refused. He looked as if he was in complete shock.

"I don't understand," he yelled.

"Stop talking and drive!" I commanded.

I realized that after traveling around for about twenty minutes that I could still hear the voices wanting to kill me, which made me even more paranoid.

He refused to drive me back and said, "But these guys are waiting for you."

"Don't you get it?" I asked. "I'm not stupid. In fact, pull over right here."

I got out of the truck and started walking down the freeway. I had no idea where I was or how to get back. I began going the direction we had driven from, and I started to realize that we had traveled for so long to get to that point that it was going to take me two or three days to walk back. Even though I was out of the car and away from the house where we parked, I still didn't feel safe. I kept thinking that because I didn't go into the house that they might try to find me. I was suspicious of every car that drove past me.

I had been walking for almost two hours when I began getting tired. I noticed that a car had pulled over up ahead. Maybe it was them, or maybe it was someone who just pulled over for whatever reason. As I got closer to the vehicle, I prepared myself to be attacked if, in fact, it was them.

As I approached the car, the window went down and a man said, "Do you want a ride?"

At first, I just ignored him, but then, he began driving along the side of me saying, "Excuse me, do you want a ride? I am going the same way."

I started thinking that I did have a long walk ahead, so I got in, and he began to drive. At first, he was on his phone, and I began hearing the voices saying that he picked me up because he wanted sex. The demons began saying to make advances towards him.

A few minutes later, he hung up his phone and said, "What's your name?"

"Eli," I told him.

"Where are you going?" he asked.

"Oakley," I replied.

"How do you get there?" he questioned.

I told him, "I don't know. I'm lost."

I didn't want to tell him anything about what just happened for fear that he might say to get out. The whole time we were talking, I was trying to figure out in my perverted mind a way to initiate physical contact with him.

I asked him, "Why did you pick me up?"

"That's a funny question," he responded.

He went on to tell me that he was a pastor and that he was on his way to convention in a town that was in a different direction from Oakley. But as he was driving, God spoke to him and said that if he didn't pick me up, no one would. He said that he didn't know where Oakley was, but that we could find it together. Hearing him say that he was being obedient to God, the demons only screamed louder.

They told me to make moves on him because that was really why he picked me up. And for the rest of the time, I sat and restrained myself. After listening and arguing with the demons about two and a half hours, he finally found Oakley and dropped me off.

After that, I stayed in a car that belonged to a guy I knew. Sometimes, this man would come out in the middle of the night to make sure that I was o.k. and to bring me food. Often, he would talk to me about God; he even gave me a Bible.

I put the Bible aside and thought, "I don't have anything to say to you, God."

I was always on the go, so I left the car and never returned.

Like Speakers All Over the World!

It was a routine day, and I partying with some friends. I was trying to figure out how to go pick up some more drugs. One of the guys had a vehicle, so I asked him if he could give me a ride. I promised that I would get him high. After returning from getting the drugs, we decided to go to his place. He lived in a modest trailer in a small trailer court near the Antioch Bridge.

When we entered the trailer, I didn't really notice anything, as I was focusing on getting high. He asked me to make a pipe on his stove. It's not really possible to make a pipe on a stove, but we were desperate. So I tried. I was facing the stove, and he was sitting on the table in back of me. I was already extremely paranoid because of my own issues, but I heard a cracking noise as if someone was walking in the hallway. It was the same sound that I heard when he walked into the room earlier. I looked at him and asked who else was there.

He smiled and said, "What do you mean?"

I said that someone had just walked down the hall. He disagreed, but I insisted on it. It only took a small noise to trigger all the paranoia in my mind, and I was convinced. But a strange feeling came over me like we weren't alone. A fear came upon me that I couldn't shake. With one eye, I pretended to be watching the pipe on the stove, but I positioned myself so that I could also see the hallway. I was expecting someone to run out and attack me. From an angle, I thought I saw him talking to someone in the hall, but there was no sound coming out of his mouth. That was another sign that something was wrong. In my mind, I was trying to figure out a way to get to the door and escape, but it was like I was frozen, and I could feel a presence around me. I couldn't explain what was going on, but there was definitely something in that trailer with us. When I looked at the guy, he just glanced at me with a smile on his face. But I could tell that there was something that was not right about him. I insisted that I couldn't make the pipe and that I wanted to leave. I slowly stepped closer to the door.

It was then that he stood up and said, "Wait, the neighbor has a pipe. I'll go get it. Sit down. I'll be right back."

I sat down on the couch because it was closest to the door. The man had a dog, which was a mid-sized black and brown mutt. The dog moved closer, and then, he stood right in front of me. He bared his teeth, growled, and started to pace back and forth as if he was making sure that I stayed in place.

I looked at the dog and was thinking, "All right, the dog ain't right either."

I didn't know if he would bite me or not, but I knew that I couldn't leave that chair for fear that he would attack me. At the same time I was tripping about the dog, I saw a shadow in the hallway from the corner of my eye. Then, I heard the floor creak. I knew someone else was in that trailer; I could feel the presence of something evil. Again, I felt a coma-like fear, and I wanted to run out the door, but I literally could not move. When the man came back into the trailer, the dog walked back and lied down in the corner.

Before I could think, I was running out the trailer, and the guy ran after me crying, "Hey, what's going on?"

I explained in a frantic voice that there was something wrong with his trailer: that something evil lived in there. I could feel it!

I tried to convince him, "Come-on. Let's get out of here! It's not safe!"

I remember trying to shake him because he didn't understand me. But he said that he couldn't leave because his dog was in there. That was their home.

As he turned to go back in, I yelled to him, "No! Don't go in there. The Devil is in there!"

He looked at me, smiled, and said, "Nobody is in there."

Then the lights in the back half of the trailer began to flash off and on.

"See? I told you!" I cried.

He said, "No, that's my dog."

"Your dog?" I yelled. "How could your dog be switching the lights off and on? If you want to go back in there, that's up to you. I'm leaving!"

I began to run away in complete fear. I found an old bike lying outside one of the trailers, so I grabbed it and rode off as fast as I could down the highway. That was about 11:00 p.m.

All of a sudden, I heard a voice. A very loud voice, like thunder.

I looked back into the darkened, evening sky. A ribbon of rust stretched across the horizon, and there was just enough glow to illuminate the orange-red clouds. There was a partial outline of the moon, and the stars shone brightly on a backdrop of charcoal black.

The voice was very loud and clear. It was kind of like the sound of a trumpet falling from the sky. "YOU BELONG TO ME AND I AM NEVER GOING TO LET YOU GO. YOU CAN RUN AS FAR AND AS FAST AS YOU CAN, BUT I'M ALREADY THERE WAITING FOR YOU WHEREVER YOU GO!!!!"

The voice came from behind me. I tried to ride the bike faster and faster to get away from it, but it was just as loud when I was further down the road as it was before. The sound encompassed me everywhere I went. I could not escape it. It was like there were speakers all over the world! At the time, I thought it was the Devil. But later, I realized that it was God talking to me with a voice that sounded like a trumpet!

Two weeks later, I went back to see the man in the trailer. To my surprise, the trailer had been demolished, and men were throwing scraps of the metal onto a pile. What happened to the man, I don't know. He was gone. I never found out where he went or what happened to him or his dog.

I was sitting next to a fence, and I heard voices; seven of them. It was like a rumbling, like there was a fight. Since there was nobody around, I assumed that the voices were coming from the other side of the fence. So I looked over to see who was fighting, but there was no one there. Among the voices, I could hear one defending me. The others were talking about killing me, but the one voice fought for me. I could hear thrashing and smashing noises. It was like the sound of a violent battle.

In my confused, perverted mind, I thought that the man wanted to sleep with me. Later, after my conversion, I was reminded of how much God hates sin and in this case, homosexuality; not the people, but the sin. The men in Sodom and Gomorrah wanted to have sex with the visiting angels. And, similar to how these cities and their residents were destroyed, God could have so easily destroyed me. But He did not. He chose to save me out of my living hell so that I could fulfill the purpose of my life.

Betty

I found myself questioning God, "Why? Why me? What is it about me that you despise so much all through life? I cried out to you to help me."

I was puzzled and confused. My thoughts took me back to when I was a child and crying out to my father to love me.

However, he would push me away and say, "But you're not my son."

As I was walking one day, I heard someone call my name. As I approached a house, I noticed a woman calling me. It was a lady I will call Betty. I used to party with her and others when I was younger. But I hadn't seen her in years. She invited me in. She was living in a camper in the back yard with her husband. As I walked in the camper, I noticed it was packed with all their belongings. That included two adult dogs and seven puppies! Newspapers were everywhere.

"Watch your step!" she exclaimed as I carefully navigated around the floor.

She said that dogs were everywhere and so were their droppings. She cleared off a place for me to sit, and I did. Most people would not have understood the way in which they lived, but to me, it was a palace. I must have dozed off, but when I woke up, Betty served me a hot plate of food and dessert. I felt like a king.

Betty used to call me "Sweety". That was a nickname that my mother gave me when I was a baby. Actually, it was kind of funny, because as I got older, people that had known me all my life called me that. But if you looked at me, that is the last thing that you would want to call me.

Here is Betty's account:

"When Sweety started coming by, he seemed to always be on the go, not staying long: a fast hit and run. But to me in my eyes, he looked really tired. He walked as if his feet were blistered and hurt. At the time, I was staying in a camper shell outside. I would tell him just kick back. At first, he would just for an hour or so. Then later, he would rest.

"He felt that he had to repay me, so he would start doing yard work. So, I'd ask what he'd like to eat. He would always say peanut butter and jelly. I would try to get him to eat something better, but no, he insisted on a pj sandwich.

"Then he started coming by more often. I felt bad. I told him that there was nowhere on Highway 4 to hide. He just walked back and forth. He needed to sleep and rest for as long as it took. He never asked me for anything, but in reality, he needed a shower, clean clothes, and a few days to catch up on eating to build up his strength, sleep, and to clear his mind.

"Sweety eventually started to listen and would stay a bit longer, but he still felt like he needed to repay me by doing work around the house."

For the next month or so, Betty opened up the camper for me, allowing me to clean up and eat. Little by little, I became a human being again.

A Vision

I had a vision of a building while walking down the street. When I went in, I saw some stairs leading up to a coffin that was resting on the top landing. The room was entirely dark, but lights were shining down onto the casket, capturing my mom and my sister who were standing nearby. They were crying.

"What's the matter? Why are you crying? Who's in there?" I cried.

There was no response.

Then, I asked, again. And again, there was no answer. Finally, I gently pushed them to see if they would acknowledge me. But they did not. I walked up the stairs to see who was in the coffin. Then, I looked in and gasped in disbelief. I was horrified! It was me!

Later, I realized that God was telling me that he was giving me notice. If I didn't give my life to Him and allow Him to change me, I was going to die. It also may have meant that the old person in me was going to die and that a new one would be born.

Even though I was angry at God, that never really stopped me from crying out to Him. And I couldn't understand why God would leave me in such a dark world, even after He saw all my pain and heard my cries all these years.

And as I got older, I began telling Him, "You know, God. If you care anything at all about me, please at least kill me and put me out of my misery."

Later, God revealed to me that He was always close and that His timing is perfect. He knew when I would be ready to yield to Him. In the meantime, life was one unpleasant experience after another. I had spent so much time on the streets that the world became secondary. I could see people, but I was stuck in this imaginary world, and I would travel back and forth. I was a prisoner in my own mind.

There were times when I would follow the creek that went through town because I thought I could hear people trying to kill my sister by drowning her.

I would run back and forth along the levee all night in a panic screaming, "Where are you? I'm coming!"

But I could never find her. Or if I was walking down the street and a car would pass me, I would get a strange feeling that my sister was trapped in the trunk. I would begin to chase the car, but I was no match for the vehicle and soon it would disappear. I would get the feeling that I would never see my sister again. The thought of how they were going to kill her bombarded my mind, and there was nothing that I could do. But after a few days, I would see her again.

When my mom and sister pulled over after seeing me on the road, I would see my sister and say, "Oh, you're o.k." with relief.

She had no idea what I was talking about, but that didn't matter.

My horrible life continued the same way it always was until…

I Heard the Voice Again

It was Easter Sunday, but it was just like any other day to me. I was thirty-three, and as I often did, I was walking along Highway 4 at Cypress. It was around noon.

And then I heard a voice saying, "TURN AWAY".

It was a soft, quiet voice but with a power that shook me to my core.

"What?" I questioned. "Who is talking to me? Turn away from what?"

The voice struck through my heart like a knife. I know I was the person the voice was addressing, and this time, I knew that the voice was God.

I knew that the "TURN AWAY" had to do with my lifestyle and my going down the wrong path.

Suddenly, pictures of my life started to flash through my mind: pictures of my mother, pictures of church and of me being saved. Bam, bam, bam. That fast. People get flashbacks of their life before they die, but the pictures that went through my mind were of the future.

Again, the voice exclaimed, "TURN AWAY!" and it was then that I broke and began to cry as I ran and screamed wildly down the street.

It was a miracle. It was a divine intervention; it was Jesus Himself. It was as if He reached over and touched me, ending the life long battle that was once my life. Suddenly, I began to run away while chains broke off. Generational curses fell away, demons and unclean spirits began to come out, and Satan himself lost the grip that he had always used to suffocate the life out of me. I was once lost, blind, and confused, but suddenly, I was running away with Jesus and in my right mind. The dark cloud dissipated, and my eyes opened and allowed me to see. I was able to hear, and in a blink of an eye, I was set free. God took away my hurt and pain, and He took my hand and called my name.

As I look back at that day, I often wonder when I was being touched by Jesus and what I could have seen, because something left my body at that time and I can only imagine what it was.

I wasn't that far away, so I ran to Mary's house and banged on the door. There was a man that was staying with her and her husband at the time.

"I will never forget the look on Eli's face!" the man recalled. "It was like he was desperate, shocked."

He ran back in to get Mary.

When she came to the door, she took one look at me and calmly said, "It's time."

"What is she saying?" I thought to myself. "Time for what?"

Mary knew that in spite of the horrible, addictive life style I was leading, I would come to know the Lord. For someone to look at me and see the terrible shape I was in, they never would have believed that I would ever turn to

God. But Mary knew. Mary knew that "with God, nothing is impossible", and she had been praying with faith that I would become a Christian. She had been waiting for the time it would happen. She just didn't know when.

I went in, sat on the couch, and told the story. Then, she called her pastor at the Spanish church in Walnut Creek to tell him that I was coming there for services at 3:00. Willy Franco was the pastor in a Spanish church called Cantu Nuevo that was held at the Hillside Covenant Church in Walnut Creek.

The house was in Oakley, and it took about 45 minutes to travel to Walnut Creek. Mary's husband had already left about one half hour before. She didn't go with him, because she wasn't quite ready. She said that her hair wasn't in place, so she decided to go later. If she had gone with her husband, she would have missed me coming to the door. Everyone thought that that in itself was a miracle. Anything that God orchestrates is a miracle.

My mother had been planning to go to a family bar-b-que, but she thought, "How can I go somewhere, eat, and have fun when my son is on drugs, losing his mind, and is living on the streets?"

So she decided to stay home. But my sister had decided to go to the party, and she was just pulling away when Mary called on her cell.

She answered, and Mary asked, "Can I speak to your mother?"

My sister drove back into the driveway and gave the phone to my mother.

See what I mean about God's perfect timing?

When my mother answered the phone, Mary said, "I have your son here, and he's crying. He wants you to come with him to church."

Mom agreed to go to church, and someone came over and picked her up. My mother said that God had spoken to her, too.

He told her, "You have lost one son, but I am giving you back your other son."

She had been in a twelve-year depression because of my brother's murder. Now she was free from this mental state and was able to go on with her life. No doubt the whole thing must have puzzled my mother. Maybe she thought it was a trick. Maybe she didn't hear it all right. It just wasn't logical that the name of God and I were even used in the same sentence.

When it was time to go to church, I got in the car with Mary. I had heard God's voice, but I was still confused. I became afraid to be in God's presence, moreover I was scared to go to church. I was scared because I was going to have to let down the walls in my life and changes were going to happen. I had built a fortress around myself for protection, and as the years went by, the walls got thicker and thicker until I had become locked inside, a prisoner of my own mind. Change was hard for me, because I was used to the world I was in. But I knew that I had to let my guard down and stand before God. Even though I was frightened and had a lot of questions, I was willing to walk out of the darkness and into the light.

I didn't know it, but I was in the battle of my life, rather, my soul. As we were driving on the large curving portion of the 680 in Walnut Creek, another voice told me to jump out.

This voice began to say, "You don't know where they are taking you or what they will do to you when you get there. You're running out of time. This is your last chance. Open the door and jump out!"

I was so confused. I had one voice telling me to turn away, showing pictures of my life, and another telling me to jump out and kill myself. I was completely drained, beat up, and worn down. This tug of war had gone on for way too long.

I later realized that the other voice was Satan and that it was his last ditch effort to kill me so that I could join him before I turned myself over to God. I don't think I would have had a problem jumping from the car because I was in such a confused and painful state, but like the time when I was on the over crossing, I couldn't move! My mind was telling me to do something, but my body wouldn't move. It was like I was paralyzed. After what seemed like an eternity of a ride, we finally arrived at the church.

Just before I went into the sanctuary of the church, I pulled a broken bottle out of my pocket that I was carrying around for protection.

"Give it to me. You won't be needing that anymore," Mary remarked as she took it and threw it in the trash can and walked away.

Suddenly, it seemed so clear. All of my hate, pain, addiction, sexual immorality, confusion, and everything that was destructive no longer had power or control over me. Like Mary had disposed of the bottle and left, so I was able to rid of all the hindrances in my life and walk away.

When I entered into the church, they were showing "The Passion of the Christ" in Spanish. Afterwards, an altar call was given in Spanish. Because I do not understand Spanish that well, Mary more or less interpreted what was said.

After explaining it to me, she said, "Come on, let's go."

And she walked with me to the front of the church. There at the altar, the pastor prayed for me and led me in a prayer where I confessed that I believed that Jesus is Lord and Savior and that He died for me, and I asked forgiveness for my sins. Then, I invited Him into my life. My prayer went something like this:

"Dear Lord,

"I believe that you are my Lord and Savior and that you died for my sins. Please forgive me for all my sins. Come into my life and guide me from now on."

It was as simple as that. Yet, sincere. Right then, there was the freedom from all the burdens I had been carrying around. Talk about rush! From the time I was on the street and heard God's voice until when church was over, I was on a spiritual high. It was much better than anything drugs could ever give.

From the time I heard God's voice to the time I was at the altar, it was like a time of contraction, labor, and then birth. It was a spiritual birth. I was reborn and now I was able to be the man God called and created me to be.

We left the church, and Mary and her husband invited my mother and I to dinner. We enjoyed a big steak supper, and we had a good time of fellowship together.

My mother was staying with my sister and her husband at the time. After I was saved, people from the church surrounded them. In the same way that people I knew used to come over to buy and sell drugs, pastors and church members flowed into our lives like a river. Church folks would come over and ask if they could pray for them. And Bible studies, encouragement, and support were everywhere. No family or no person is too far removed from God's love. God wants to raise up people out of the darkness of the streets.

Then, they discussed what they were going to do with me. In the past when I was coming off of drugs, I used to scream and throw things when I was at home. My mother said that they did not want to have to go through that anymore, and she said that I should go to a hospital to get cleaned up.

But I didn't want to go. And I never really had to go to the hospital. I went home and stayed with my mother and sister.

However, the next morning, Mary found a men's home in Pittsburg. It is a place where men can recover from drugs or alcohol and start a new life with God. Mary picked me up, took me to some stores, and bought me some clothes. Then, she drove me to the home.

When I got there, I put my things down on one of the beds. Residents were just coming in from their jobs. One of them became very upset that I had taken his bed. So, I moved to a different bed, and stayed there one night.

But God spoke to me again. "I want you to get your things and leave. I don't need you to be where people can't see you. I need for you to be out on the streets so that you can tell them what I have done for you."

It reminded me of the time that Jesus healed the man that was possessed by demons and was set free. The man wanted to go with Jesus, but Jesus told him to go home and to tell the people what God had done from him.

I had only been to my sister's house once and that was when I was recovering from the head injury. So I didn't remember exactly where it was. But the one visit was enough. Family members told me that I would have to leave because of all the potential trouble that always followed me. When I left the men's home, I got on a bus. I wound up in front of Wal-Mart. I remembered that my sister lived somewhere in one of the many houses behind that store. I really was in a fog after I was hit in the head, but the area looked familiar to me. I got off the bus and started walking. I turned left, then right, then on and on, left, right, etc., and amazingly I went right to my sister's house. I recognized the tree out in front. It was absolutely amazing that I got on the bus that would take me to a store and then be able to find the right house. Well, God had orchestrated it all. My mother just happened to be there at the time.

As I walked up to the house, I found that the front door was open so I went right in. I walked though the house and into my mom's room where she was standing with a big smile. She still had not seen me, but she looked so peaceful and without worry that I could only imagine that her fears of me overdosing or being killed were no longer controlling her. Then, she looked up and saw me.

"What are you doing here?" Mom cried. "You are supposed to be at the men's home!"

When she looked at me, her smile left, not because she wasn't happy to see me, but because she thought, "Oh, no. Here we go again."

You see, it was part of the miracle that God was doing, because in everyone's mind, it was impossible for me to change everything. It would take years of help. And, in fact, it was impossible for me to change, "But with God, all things are possible."

"God told me to leave," I replied.

Just then, my sister walked in, saw me, and said, "You can't stay here!"

Then, she walked away.

I asked them to give me one more chance to show that I had changed, but they did not agree. They thought that I was making excuses to get high again. So they called Mary.

Mary felt a responsibility for me, and she felt that she had to do whatever it took to take care of me until I could start a new life on my own. So they had another discussion, but this time on the phone. They agreed to let me stay at my sister's home if Mary would pick me up every morning to get me away from the house. And that is what she did for nine and a half months.

Mary picked me up, and then she fed me, helped me study the Bible, and took me places that I had never been able to go to before such as the beach, museums, etc. She even took me on a field trip with her daughter's school to see a play in Stockton. Some of the kids from the school recognized me as being the man on the street. They asked Mary's daughter if I was her father.

She answered, "No. That's my mom's friend."

I was grateful that I was able to see many of the things I had never experienced before. I was so excited and so full of new life that I took every opportunity to speak to everyone about my divine intervention. I told people that I knew and those that I didn't, people on the streets, those in stores, everywhere.

While I was out with Mary, I pulled out a cigarette. I had been saving it for about a week. She asked why I still smoked: was I nervous or did I feel like it was an addiction?

She said, "When Jesus delivered you, he delivered you completely and that every time you smoked, it was like you were reaching back in God's hand and saying, 'But God, I want to keep this one.'"

As I stood there, I thought about Jesus on the cross and every great thing He had done for me. I didn't want to disrespect God. I quickly put out the cigarette and never smoked again.

It was a twenty year addiction to cigarettes, and all I had to do was to say, "Here God. You can have it back!"

I continued to be prayed over by pastors and leaders who worked in spiritual warfare. There were times when I would vomit and scream wildly like in an exorcism. Well, I am sure it was. I remember something inside me felt like it was clawing from the inside of me as it rose up and out of me. Dripping in sweat and aching from head to toe, I felt like I was run over by a train.

God later revealed that He could have delivered me all at once, but that He had to do it a little bit at a time or I could not have handled it. I was too far gone; there was that much sin and too many demons. God ripped them out of my life, bit by bit. And when that happened, He cured my mental illness, my drug addiction, and more.

Whenever I Speak

I continued to go to church and to study the Bible and pray. I got a job and housing. And I have had wonderful opportunities to speak at various churches, community groups, and Christian radio programs, sharing my testimony about the miraculous way that God drew me out of a very destructive life style and that he delivered me so that I can serve Him.

My goal is to help others who are caught up in horrendous demonic captivity and the related world of drugs, homosexuality, prostitution, and homelessness, not to mention the resulting mental illness, by telling them that there is hope. There is deliverance. And it is available to them. It is through Jesus Christ. And He is just waiting to be able to deliver anyone who calls on His name.

After telling my story at various places, invariably people would come up to me afterwards.

"I was looking at a mirror," some people confessed as they came up to me, one by one.

Grown men were crying. All of a sudden wounds were open, and people were dealing with new convictions. Some were brought back to my age, and they knew that they needed to deal with things that happened in their lives.

"You were talking about my life."

People from all walks of life, even pastors, have come to me in tears.

"My son or daughter is lost in that world. You have given me hope that my prayers will be answered, and he or she will come back to God. What God has done for you, He will do in my kid's life!"

My life and this story was put together by God for a purpose. What I lived was a nightmare. I was very close to dying so many times. I should be dead now: AIDS, drug overdose, suicide attempt, and murder. I had tried to escape reality, and drugs did that for me. But they brought me down to the very pit of existence. Until I was set free. I can't take credit for my deliverance. It was God who brought me out of all this and allowed me to live for His glory. I couldn't have done it myself.

After I was saved, people used to ask, "Why you?" Why were you delivered from all the evil you were in and others weren't?"

I asked the question myself. "Why me? Why was I chosen to live this awful life and then be set free from all that was holding me down and would have eventually killed me."

I visited a church, and during the service, the Lord spoke to me. He said that someone had a word for me. After the sermon, I went up front for prayer. The pastor spoke to me and said that he wasn't going to say words but that he was going to put his arms around me. When he did, he said that it would be the Holy Spirit holding me though his body. And when he reached over and hugged me, I began to cry loudly for about ten minutes. Afterwards, the pastor asked me why I reacted the way I did. I told him it was because the Lord spoke to me and said this was how the world was supposed to hold me, with purity, love, and compassion, and giving to my spirit; not taking away from it. That was the way that I always wanted my dad to embrace me in fatherly love.

After I was saved, I began asking Him questions.

One of my inquiries was, "If you were able to save me, why did you wait so long to do it?"

God responded, "There were things out there in the world that you needed to learn that you can't learn in a book."

He also said, "Even though you thought that you were walking away from me for thirty-three years, you never left my sight."

He even gave me a vision of seven bridges that led to a city. The city was in ruins and the bridges were destroyed. I knew in my mind that there was no turning back. Ever since my conversion, my Divine intervention, my experience with Jesus has been a constant learning experience. Just like a baby, I had to learn how to walk, eat, and even love. It took two years for me to learn how to sleep without my shoes on and almost three years to be able to sleep in a house. For a long time, I had to sleep with the door open or next to a window in order to get out quick if I needed to. But God has been faithful, patient, and merciful.

Even though God had delivered me from my demons and had shown me so much in my life, there was one thing that I was having trouble letting go of. Even though I walked away from the homosexual lifestyle, my mind would race with thirty-three years of memories and the only lifestyle I knew. I fought, struggled, and had wars in my mind night and day. The easiest way to explain it is if one day a person woke up and someone told him or her that they were the opposite sex. It would be very difficult to process that. I guess that homosexuality was my Goliath, but I have trusted and believed God and held Him to His word.

There was no logical way to defeat him in my mind, so I prayed.

"God, I don't know how you will conquer this giant, but I know that you can."

One day, I visited a friend of mine whom I used to sleep with. I was looking forward to telling him how my experience with Jesus had changed my life.

But then he tried to approach me sexually.

I stopped him and said, "I'm not that person anymore!"

The Holy Spirit said, "It's time to go."

I turned around, got in my car, and before I could drive away, I began to weep because God had done the impossible and defeated my Goliath. There is nothing too big for God! Not too long after that, the same guy called and invited me over to tell him about Jesus.

I should have died a number of times. Miraculous things happened to me all along the way. Quite a few of my acquaintances are incarcerated or dead. But God was merciful to me, and He had and still has a plan for my life. No doubt someone had been praying for me.

I have told God, "Thank you for allowing me to go through such darkness, and with my own eyes, witness Him turn it all to light."

A lady once told me that I influenced people to do wrong. I showed people another way of life; helping them to turn their lives into ones of bondage and addiction. I showed them drugs and prostitution, and I invited them into a world of darkness. Anyone who came around me turned into a drug addict or a slave to darkness.

Then she prophesized, "There were so many you took down into that horrible world, but God can turn that around. And more will be influenced to come to Him by your testimony and your book than those who were influenced by you for bad."

Wherever I Go

Now it seems as if everywhere I go, people stare at me, trying to figure out if I was that horrible person they once saw walking along the street. Others don't even recognize me.

Once I actually went back to my old street to tell people how God changed me. I walked up to one house, and the man came out.

I told him who I was, and he said, "Who?"

I repeated my name.

He said, "That's not you! If you are the same guy, God has really done a number on you!"

About a half a dozen people have actually come up to me after my conversion and told me that they had been praying for me back when I was walking along the streets and talking to myself. I could be in my work clothes and dirty, and people would still notice the big change in me.

One time I was down at the roadside store at Cypress and Highway 4. I saw a man whom I recognized. He used to be a drug dealer with whom I did business. As he walked by, he looked at me, and looked again. Then, it finally dawned on him who I was.

He said, "I thought I recognized you."

I knew a girl whom I will call "Erica". Erica lived on the streets with her girlfriend "Terry". Erica went to prison, but not before she turned her seventeen-year-old girlfriend out. All alone, Terry was addicted and on the streets. She thought that if she broke the law, she would be able to go to prison to be with Erica. So she broke into a random house and stabbed a lady in the face twenty-seven times. She told me that at one point, the knife broke off, but she kept on stabbing with what was left in her hand. Terry was arrested, but she didn't go to prison; she went to the California Youth Authority. Years later, I was reunited with Terry.

As she looked at me, she exclaimed, "I know God exists now because I'm looking at a miracle!"

After I became a Christian, I went back to my friend Betty and told her how the Lord changed my life.

Betty wrote the previous account and continued:

> "One day, he told me about a lady that stopped him on Highway 4 and told him that she had been praying for him. That day changed his life, because two to three days later, he disappeared for a few weeks, took himself to rehab, left there. But he committed himself to our Father God."

Once, I walked into a church when a pastor was speaking. All of a sudden, he stopped talking and cried, "Are you the man I think you are?"

"Who do you think I am?" I replied.

"Are you the man who used to walk up and down the street screaming at people who weren't there?"

"Yes, that was me."

"Every single time you would walk by my shop, I would pray that God would rescue you. I put out my hand and prayed for you. I knew that you were fighting with demons," the pastor said.

Another man told me that whenever he saw me on the streets, he not only prayed for me, but he even told his kids to reach out their hands to me and pray that God would turn my life around and touch my life.

I received a letter from a guy whom I had known from years before. In his letter he said that as he sat inside the prison walls, he looked back at the person I used to be. He saw a man that was lost and sick, hopeless and without a reason to live. He remembered that one day, I walked up to him on the street with a Bible in my hand and began to share what God had done for me.

As he compared the old me to the new me, he wrote, "Every time I think of you, you make it impossible for me to say that God does not exist."

There was one time that some people and I went to pray for a man. He wasn't home, but some others invited us in this house that was used for partying and other things. As we walked in, everyone got up and stepped away from us until they were all standing in the corner. These were all people that I either used to party with or were living the same type of lifestyle.

We asked if anyone wanted prayer.

"No," they responded.

"Why not?" the church people asked.

They said that they were afraid of prayer.

When asked why they were afraid of it, one of the guys in the corner said, "Because look what it did to our old friend!"

One time when I was 34, I was in San Ramon. When I came out of a building, a garbage man, who was picking up the trash next door, approached me and said, "My brother needs a job. I was wondering if you know if they are hiring here."

I told him to come inside and that I would give him the boss's phone number. He did, but he kept staring at me.

Finally, he blurted out, "Is that you, Brother? Are you the man who lives across the hill and walked along the street screaming at people who weren't there?

"God once told me to park the car and tell you how much He loved you," he continued. "But when I got out of the car, approached, and looked into your eyes, it was if I was looking at Satan himself. I couldn't do it. So, I went back to my car, and told God that I just couldn't talk to you."

The man started to cry, because he realized that I was the crazy man out on the street who was lost in a horrible world.

"I am sorry that I left you out there like that," he cried, "but I just couldn't talk to you."

"Brother, it's o.k. God still did it", I reassure him. "God brought me out of it."

A friend of mine whom had known me for years was listening to the conversation and said, "You're the one that God has chosen."

I happened to see an old friend of mine. We used to get high together. I approached her and told her that I was thinking about her and wanted to invite her to church. She stood there in unbelief. She said that she had just had a dream about me and that I was walking down the street. She didn't see my face, but she knew that it was me.

In her dream she yelled, "Hey, wait for me. Take me with you."

To me, this was saying that I was on my way to heaven and that she wanted to come along, too.

A friend of mine told me that someone whom I had known named "Alex" had died of AIDS. Alex was the teenager who was trying to speak to his mother on the phone. He died seven or eight years after I saw him in San Francisco when he was trying to call home.

My mother was always there for me. She cared for me, prayed for me, and other than what she did not know about my father's behavior, she protected me. God gave me a revelation that I was walking in complete darkness. Up ahead were flames and fire. I was in a trance and was headed towards them. I glanced back and saw my mother following behind me at a distance. In the darkness, she put her hands in front of her trying to feel her way as if she were blind.

Then, she had a conversation with the Devil saying, "I don't care how far into hell I have to follow my son, but I'm not leaving without him."

And she has certainly done that. She followed me from place to place into the most hideous living situations and pain until she saw her prayers answered.

Since Then....

After my conversion, my mother, my aunt, and I were able to move out on our own. It was a little apartment in Antioch. It wasn't in the best area, but it was a home, and we lived there for some time. We were able to have Bible studies and have friends over. I ran into a friend of mine who was looking for a place to live. So I invited him in. Then another friend came, then another. Before I knew it, I had five guys living with us in the small apartment. These were all the men that I had partied with and lived in the streets with. They all decided to give their lives to God, and we began to see lives transformed. We all ate together, read the Bible, and went to church. Some of them slept in the living room; some even slept under the table.

One day, the pastor came over, looked around, and said, "What is all this mess?"

My mother replied, "My son keeps bringing people to live here."

One day I was giving one of the guys a ride to work, and I got pulled over. The officer was real polite, at first. After I gave him my name, however, he returned with his gun drawn and he told me to open the door and come out slowly. He said that if he found any drugs or weapons, he would take me to jail. I told him that I didn't deny who I was and that I used to be a bad person doing bad things and hanging out with bad people. But I said that I was not that guy anymore. I told him that I was a Christian. He continued to search the vehicle as more cops arrived. I said that you can look if you want; you'll only find a bunch of Bibles. The vehicle I was driving was a church van that had the church logo on all the windows and that it may look strange to people watching. But in fact, I had made a wrong turn, and I didn't have a license.

After searching the van, the officer gave me the ticket said, "I want to commend you for turning your life around."

He didn't know me, but the information on the computer in his car didn't fit the person he was standing in front of.

He said, "But I am still impounding your car."

I replied, "I understand."

He then told me how to get the van back.

And I got all the Bibles out and started walking. As I was leaving, I said, "Well, God, I don't know how you will fix this problem, but I know that you can."

I was afraid to call the pastor, but I did. He said that the police had already talked to him and that the number was on the logo in the windows. I told him what the officer told me about getting the vehicle back. He came over, and on our way home, I showed him a house that was for sale. We eventually got the van, and in the process, the pastor called a realtor about the house.

A month later, he stretched out his hand and said, "Here are the keys to that house. You guys can move in."

And that day, we started building a home for men who wanted to be rescued by God. I didn't have any skills or education on building or running a men's home, but I did have the determination and desire to see men who were lost and bound receive Jesus as their Lord and Savior. Mostly, it was learning by trial and error. Soon after the word got out, we began getting visits from pastors and even people from the community asking how they could help. It was a great experience. Months went by and opposition came. We ran into financial problems, and the home was closed. Everyone went their own way. The closing was hard to go through, but I didn't let it detour me from my relationship with God. I went back to my mom's apartment.

Soon after, my aunt began to get sick. One day, my mother and I came home and she wasn't there. My mother found that strange and started calling relatives. Sure enough, she was in the hospital.

My family gathered together in the small, cramped waiting room in the emergency room. Sirens blared outside as the ambulance rushed in with patients. The loud speaker called for Doctor So and So to report of the emergency room. Zombie-like people passed each other in the halls awaiting some news. As for us, we were praying for my aunt. She was my dear aunt whom I have mentioned several times. She had been fighting cancer for about eight years. We watched it tear her down, little by little.

We took turns visiting her in her room even though she was unconscious. They said they didn't want us to excite her. When it was my turn to visit her, I wasn't quite ready for what I saw. You see, when I walked in, I saw a silhouette of an image, and there was a calm peace. The image was standing next to my aunt, holding her hand and touching her head.

As I stood there and stared, the image said, "What do you want to do with her?"

And suddenly, I am staring into a field of tall, green grass that was swaying in the breeze. There was a huge beautiful tree with plenty of shade. The branches were moving with the rhythm of the soft wind. The sun was bright and high in the sky. And it was absolutely quiet. It was the picture of peace. And there in the center was my aunt sitting under the big tree, her hair blowing in the breeze. She was running her fingers through the grass that looked like ocean waves. I looked closer at her face. She looked like she was about ten years old. And she was full of peace and innocence. Her eyes were watering and full of life and joy.

Then, I heard the voice again.

"What do you want me to do with her?"

I realized that I was back in her hospital room, staring at her lifeless body. She was lying there hooked up to machines that were helping her breathe.

I was puzzled by the question I was asked, so I went back to told my mother who was still waiting in the other room. We talked about it and decided that we wanted her to stay with us and to get better. However, three days later, the doctors decided to get permission to turn off the life support machine. Everyone came to say their last goodbye, and some pastors came to pray her into God's arms. To everyone's surprise, when the doctor turned off the machine, she woke up and asked for a hot dog and Pepsi. Everyone was shocked, especially the doctors.

It was like a great celebration. Everybody was standing in awe, because an extension of life had been given. That evening when dinner came around, we asked the nurse to bring her supper. She said that she would have to order a special meal, because she wasn't included on the evening list.

The nurse laughed and said that she had been given a gift of time because she wasn't expected to be here for dinner.

The next day, she slipped back into a coma and was transferred to a hospice house. Our prayers changed. Before we told God that she belonged to us and that we wanted her to stay.

Now we told God, "She belongs to you. You can love her better than we can. For us to expect her to stay on this earth was only selfishness when you can take her home and heal her completely."

A day and a half later, she went home to be with the Lord.

We began cleaning out the apartment, because we couldn't afford it anymore. Basically, we got rid of everything, and we drove away from the apartment with just a few bags of clothes in a car that a sister from church blessed us with. We stayed at my older sister's house for a while. I remember one morning getting ready for church. I was opening my trunk and digging for clothes to wear.

It was then that Satan began to speak to me, "Where is your God? What has God done for you? Nothing has changed."

I automatically started to reflect on my old life. One time in particular, I was homeless, but I knew a lady.

She told me, "One day you know you are going to freeze to death out here."

"I am not that lucky," I replied.

She said that she would leave her car open and that I could put my clothes, if I have any, in the trunk. So I did.

She said, "The only thing is that you have to be out of the car by a certain time before my old man goes to work."

Her husband's son was the one who murdered my brother.

I suddenly snapped out of the daydream and began to say, "Devil, you are a liar! I've gotten a hold of Jesus, and I am not letting go! The struggle was too hard and the nightmare was too long, and I refuse to give up on the victory. Get thee behind me Satan in the name of Jesus!"

I gathered up my clothes, got ready to go to church, and had a wonderful time in the Lord. I realized that I needed to rejoice because I wasn't hungry. I wasn't on drugs. I wasn't out of my mind, and I wasn't sleeping in a bush. I am a child of the living God.

I went to Berkeley to street preach with a group of people from a local church. They had a Christian band on the corner and several small groups walking around preaching and passing out tracts. I was standing next to one of the pastors when I heard a group of people chanting and yelling out for the band to play music from a speed metal group. When I turned around, I saw a group of hardcore punk rockers with big spikes, punk clothes, and black boots. One of the guys had a tattoo of what was going to be a skull on his face.

I thought to myself, "God, how would you minister to them?"

I remembered when I was a punk rocker and rebellious. To my surprise, the pastor struck up a conversation with them, and then he said, "Eli, come here and share your testimony with these guys."

So I did. I closed my eyes and began to speak. Within a few minutes, I heard some sniffling and coughing. I opened my eyes, and they began to share how they experienced similar situations growing up.

There was a calmness, and God began to say to me, "It's just a costume."

I told them, "We all hurt the same. We all cry the same, and we all want to be loved the same."

After everyone shared and went their separate ways, God said, "That is how I would minister to them.

Once I was giving a friend a ride home when we pulled up to his house. Police officers were in the process of raiding his home. I already knew the routine all too well. I pulled over and got out of the car. They had their guns drawn and began to ask questions. When I gave them my name, they were a little surprised. Most of the local officers knew me from the past. One cop began asking questions about how much time I did. It had been about four years since I had gotten saved and basically disappeared from the streets.

I replied, "Four years," not understanding his question.

By the time more policemen surrounded me in amazement of my transformation. They thought that I had been in prison.

Another officer asked, "I heard that you changed your life. Why are you hanging out with this guy?"

"I was just giving him a ride home," I replied, but in reality, I try to never miss an opportunity to share with someone in my past about my experience with God.

The policeman questioned, "If you weren't locked up, where have you been and what happened to you?"

By this time, there were about seven or eight officers around me.

I started, "This may sound strange to you, but I was walking down the street one day, and I heard God speak to me. I was obedient to His voice, I went to church, and that day I received Jesus Christ as my Lord and Savior. And boom, here we are four years later in my right mind, clean and sober, and serving God."

The cops stood in amazement. They began sharing stories of crazy things they remembered me doing. One officer said that in all the eighteen years of being on the force, he said that he had never seen anything like me before.

"There were a few other guys who were pretty bad," he recalled, "but you were the worst. Ninety-nine percentage of the people we deal with change because of probation or the courts, but they don't last. But you did it all by yourself. You were the last person that anybody thought would make it out, but here you are!"

I replied, "Well, I can't take the credit for what you are looking at. It was a miracle from God. I was willing to lay down my life and accept the fact that I was going to hell, but from the beginning, God had another plan for my life."

I applied for a few janitorial jobs, but I couldn't pass the test to even get to an interview. And I started to think that maybe I should go back to high school so that I could get this job, but I blew it off. I thought that I could never go back to school. A few Sundays later, one of the ministers in church told me that he had a word from God that I needed to get a college education.

I received the word, but I questioned it.

"College?" I asked myself. "I can't even go back to high school."

Being the procrastinator that I was, a few weeks went by. Then someone else told me that God wanted me to have an education. A few days later, I went to another school, Independence High School in Brentwood, an independent study program for high school students and adults, and signed up. At the orientation, I looked around. All the students were there with their parents. The room was quiet, but full. The instructor came to my table and noticed that the chair next to me was empty.

She asked, "Where is your student?

I looked at her and began to sweat from nervousness. A little voice inside of my head said to run away as fast as I could and stop embarrassing myself.

"Sir, your student?" she asked again.

This time everyone was looking at me.

"I am the student," I declared.

As soon as I said that, I looked over to the next table and noticed a young woman that I went to school with. She was enrolling her high school student.

I thought to myself, "What am I doing here?"

I wanted to leave, but I shook it off.

I told myself, "If I continue to run away, I'll never be the man God has called and created me to be. I am important, and I will be somebody."

On the first day of school, I was driving my mother around taking care of some errands fore my first class. And what do you know? My car stalled thirty minutes before my appointment with my teacher. The school wasn't too far away. I spotted a lady that I knew, and I asked her for a ride. She agreed.

Mom said, "Go ahead, Son. I'll wait for you here."

On my way to school, I called a guy to take my mother home and to go look at the car. Then I arranged for my sister to pick me up from school. After the appointment, I walked out to the parking lot with an armful of books: American Government, Biology, Health, so on.

My sister took one look at me and said, "Yeh right. You'll never make it."

She was a lot younger than I was, so she only had seen me as an addict all my life. She didn't say it to be mean, but it had never been in my character to read, study, or even care about life.

I got in the car and thought, "I'll show you."

In the beginning, it was hard to study. It was really the first time in my life that I had made the effort, but I was determined. Failing or quitting was not an option. I would sit for four to five hours every day and read and read and read until it felt like the muscles in my brain were actually moving. After all, it had been fifteen years since I read a book or at least, even opened one.

I picked up a little job, and before I knew it, I had three part-time jobs. And I continued to study and go to church. I worked hard in school and made straight A's, except for Algebra. After a few months went by, the teacher said that I was chosen as "Student of the Month" for the entire school. I was told that I would receive a certificate and be allowed to share who I was in front of all the staff. When the day came, I basically told them my story and how God miraculously pulled me through. By the time I was done, the room was quiet and you could hear sniffles and an occasional cough all across the room. After I received my award, some of the teachers greeted me. Whether or not they believed in God as I did, they were deeply touched.

A week later at my next appointment with my teacher, I talked to my teacher about writing a book about my life. In fact, I told him that God said that if I went out into the world and shared what He had done for me, His people would come with open arms. It was just as I had finished telling him those things that a lady walked in the classroom. She said that she happened to be at the award ceremony and that she had heard my speech. This lady also mentioned that she didn't know if she would ever see me again because we had different schedules, but that evening, she just happened to notice that I was in the room with my teacher while she was taking a break from a class down the hall.

One of the things I had said in my speech was that I wanted to write a book about my experiences. I had thought about it, and a few people whom had heard my testimony encouraged me to do so. But I didn't think that I could. The woman told me that she was an author and that when I mentioned that I wanted to write my life story, she felt that she wanted to help. It was like an awareness from God that she should offer to assist me in this project. My teacher was a witness to what just happened before his very eyes.

About a month later, I found myself in between homes again. One morning, I walked out one door, not knowing where I was going to sleep that night and started driving. I wondered what I was going to do. I started thinking about the past and my future. One thing I knew for sure was that my worst day with Jesus was better than my best day without Him in the streets. Before the day was over, I had made a call to a Christian couple that I knew. Before I could say anything, the man said that the Lord spoke to him and told him to open his door to me to stay with him and his wife. Of course, I agreed. It was hard at first, because I really didn't know them. But they made me feel at home. I would go to work in the morning and then usually meet up with my mom and sister. We would hang out at a park all day. Sometimes, we would go to a fast food restaurant and stay all day. Then, towards evening, we would go our own way and do it all again the next day. A few weeks later, my mom was blessed with her own apartment. That made it easier for us, because we didn't have to hang out in public anymore.

For the next year, I was interviewed, and I wrote information for the book. I also continued in school until finally, I received all my credits. It was amazing that I had the mindset to go to school. It was from God. I never missed one class, and I was never late. I was able to graduate and walk in the ceremony. It was twenty years late, but better late than never. I was honored to be able to give my speech at the commencement ceremony:

"My name is Elulalio Contreras, AKA Eli, I am 37 years old, and I was scheduled to graduate in 1989. But because of situations and bad choices, my life took a turn for the worse. As a child, I suffered from abuse. As a result, I began to question my identity. When I got to high school, I was unable to fit in or make friends. So I changed my looks, and I became a hardcore punk rocker with a colorful Mohawk, big black boots, and a leather jacket. While my classmates were into sports, going to dances, and being normal, I was wondering the streets in search of the missing pieces of my life.

"In order to numb the pain and to escape reality, I turned to drugs. They soon became a big part of my life.

"I became very angry and disrespectful towards anybody in authority, which eventually got me expelled from school.

"After I left school, I went into a deep depression. For the next fourteen years, I was pretty much homeless and I lived on the streets doing whatever I had to do to survive.

"In my mind, I tried to figure out how I got to where I was a million times.

"But then I got help from God, and for the first time, I knew that I was important as a human being and that I have a purpose in life. I plan to get a degree in counseling and help the people I once was.

"If you had told me five years ago that I was going back to school, I would have laughed in disbelief. But today, I'm not only graduating, but I have been given the honor of sharing how I was able to get to this point. My speech today is for anyone who has had a dream stolen from them, for anyone who thought they would never amount to anything, or for someone who may have a son or daughter or friend who has lost their dreams. There is hope.

"Ever since I was a child, I head a voice saying that I was worthless. I would never amount to anything or accomplish anything. But today that voice is a liar!

"Thank you all of you who have had the patience to help me through this journey, and I will leave you with this. When life becomes unbearable, don't ask God to give you an easier life. Ask Him to make you a stronger person.

"And don't give up on your dreams!

Almost immediately after being saved, I started thinking about my father. I wanted to share with him what God had done for me. After all, after what God had forgiven me for, who was I to hold anger or resentment towards anyone? I started to reflect on all the sick and disturbing memories I had of my father, but I couldn't feel compassion for him.

It was then that I heard the Lord say, "I want you to forgive your father, and I want you to pray for him. I don't create people that way. Somebody hurt him when he was a child."

It was after I forgave him and prayed for him that I was able to release everything and have joy in my heart. I wrote my father a letter telling him that I forgave him and that I was praying for him. I also included a short testimony of how God restored me. I was no longer that disturbed, evil person that he saw grow up before his very eyes. I was excited when I received a letter back from him. When I opened it, he said that he didn't care about me and not to pray for him. End of letter! All my life, I tried to get this man to love me and to care about me. I wanted him to be impressed by me, and I wanted to make him proud. But with his sharp words, I lost my breath.

It was then that God said, "Son, I am your Father, and I love you."

Suddenly, it didn't seem important what the letter said.

I put it down and declared, "Dad, you might have given up on me, but I'll never stop praying for you and I'll never give up on you "

And I took the power back from the Devil.

As I thought about the words "I love you" that God said to me, I started to think about it. It was something that I desired all my life and never got. Although this may have sounded very ungrateful, I know that God understood. I told God that I knew He did the impossible for me, but if He expected me to love Him, He was going to have to show me how. I didn't know what love was.

And just like a child spends time with the parent and a relationship is formed, I feel God every moment. When I go to sleep, He tucks me in. When I wake up, I feel His arms around me. He breathes air into my body. He holds my hands and walks me though life. He provides all things and meets every need. It's indescribable. The power He holds and the unexplainable width and depth of His love is beyond our understanding. It is like I was asleep for a long time, then I was brought back from a coma. Was it real or a dream? All I have is the memories of who I used to be. I'll let those memories be a testimony of how God rescued and changed my life and all that He has done for me and through me.

The following is a prayer I wrote to God:

> *"I thank you God because when I was worthless, you saw me worthy.*
>
> *You loved me when I couldn't love myself. You rescued me from dark places, delivered me from my addictions and demons, and restored my mind. Words aren't enough and my actions are limited, but God, I love you.*
>
> *Thank you,*
> *Your son, Eli"*

References

ꟺ

For God so loved the world that He gave His one and only Son, that whoever believes in Him shall not perish, but have eternal life. John 3:16.

I am come that they might have life, and that they might have it more abundantly. John 10:10

All have sinned and fall short of the glory of God. Romans 3:23

The wages of sin is death, but the gift of God is eternal life in Jesus Christ our Lord. Romans 6:23

God demonstrates His own love toward us, in that while we were yet sinners, Christ died for us. Romans 5:8

...I am the way, and the truth, and the life: no one comes to the Father but through me. John 14:6

As many as received them, to them He gave the right to become children of God, even to those who believe in His name. John 1:12

By grace you have been saved through faith; and not of yourselves, It is the gift of God; not as a result of works, that no one should boast. Ephesians 2:8,9

If you confess with your mouth the Lord Jesus and believe in your heart that God has raised Him from the dead, you will be saved. For with the heart one believes unto righteousness, and with the mouth confession is made unto salvation. For the Scripture says, "Whoever believes on Him will not be put to shame." For there is no distinction between Jew and Greek, for the same Lord over all is rich to all who call upon Him. For "whoever calls on the name of the Lord shall be saved. Romans 10:8-13

For I know the thoughts that I think toward you, says the Lord, thoughts of peace and not evil, to give you a future and a hope. Then you will call upon me and go and pray to me, and I will listen to you. And you will seek me and find me, when you search for Me with all your heart. Jeremiah 29: 11-13

Behold I stand at the door and knock; if any one hears my voice and opens the door, I will come into him. Revelation 3:20

You intended to harm me, but God intended it for good to accomplish what is now being done, the saving of many lives. Genesis 50:20

For he has rescued us for the dominion of darkness and brought us into the kingdom of the Son he loves, in whom we have redemption, the forgiveness of sins. Colossians 1:13

Therefore, if anyone is in Christ, he is a new creation; old things have passed away; behold, all things have become new. II Corinthians 5:16-18

Ask and it will be given to you; seek and you will find; knock and the door will be opened to you. For everyone who asks receives, he who seeks finds; and to him who knocks, the door will be opened. Matthew 7: 7-8

For God did not give us a spirit of timidity, but a spirit of power, of love, and of self-discipline. So do not be ashamed to testify about our Lord, or ashamed of me his prisoner. But join with me in suffering for the gospel, but the power of God who has saved us and called us to a holy life not because of anything we have done but because of his own purpose and grace. This grace was given us in Christ Jesus before the beginning of time. II Timothy 1: 7-9

For those who have been born again, not of perishable seed, but of imperishable, through the living and enduring word of God. I Peter 1:23

To this you were called, because Christ suffered for you, leaving you an example, that you should follow in his steps... He himself bore our sins inhis body on the tree, so that we might die to sins and live for righteousness; by his wounds you have been healed. I Peter 2:21, 24.

Therefore, if anyone is in Christ, he is a new creation; old things have passed away; behold, all things have become new. II Corinthians 5:17

...not knowing that the goodness of God leads you to repentance? Romans 2:4

Jesus answered them, "Most assuredly, I say to you, whoever commits sin is a slave to sin. And a slave does not abide in the house forever, but a son abides forever. Therefore, if the Son makes you free, you shall be free indeed. John 8:34-36

Knowing this, that our old man was crucified with Him, that the body of sin might be done away with, that we should no longer be slaves of sin. For he who has died has been freed from sin. Romans 6:6-7

But now having been set free from sin, and having become slaves of God, you have your fruit to holiness, and to the end, eternal life. Romans 6:22

...at that time you were without Christ, being aliens from the commonwealth of Israel and strangers from the covenants of promise, having no hope and without God in the world. But now in Christ Jesus you who once were far off have been brought near by the blood of Christ. Ephesians 2:12-13

Therefore, since we are surrounded by such a great could of witnesses, let us throw off everything that hinders and the sin that so easily entangles, and let us run with perseverance the race marked out for us.
Let us fix our eyes on Jesus, the author and perfector of our faith, who for the joy set before him endured the cross, scorning it's shame, and sat down at the right hand of the throne of God. Hebrews 12:1-2

Do you not know that the unrighteous will not inherit the kingdom of God? Do not be deceived. Neither fornicators, nor idolaters, nor adulterers, nor homosexuals, nor sodomites, nor thieves, nor covetous, nor drunkards, nor revilers, nor extortioners will inherit the kingdom of God. And such were some of you. But you were washed, but you were sanctified, but you were justified in the name of the Lord Jesus and by the Spirit of our God. I Corinthians 6:8-11

And the God of all grace who called you to his external glory in Christ, after you have suffered a little while, will himself restore you and make you strong, firm, and steadfast. I Peter 5:10

Blessed are those who wash their robes, that they may have the right to the tree of life...Revelation 22:14

He who overcomes will inherit all this, and I will be his God and he will be my son. Revelation 21:7

My eyes will watch over them for their good, and I will bring them back to this land. I will build them up and not tear them down. I will plant them and not uproot them. I will give them a heart to know me, that I am the Lord. They will be my people, and I will be their God, for they will return to me with all their heart. Jeremiah 24:6,7

CPSIA information can be obtained at www.ICGtesting.com
Printed in the USA
BVOW09s0447280214

346288BV00002B/3/P